Lorraine Hansberry

A RAISIN
IN THE SUN

THE BARNARD BIOGRAPHY SERIES

LORRAINE HANSBERRY

Award-Winning Playwright and Civil Rights Activist

Susan Sinnott

Foreword by Thulani Davis

CONARI PRESS
Berkeley, California

Conari Press books are distributed by Publishers Group West.

Cover illustration by Lisa Falkenstern.

Library of Congress Cataloging-in Publication Data

Sinnott, Susan
    Lorraine Hansberry : award-winning playwright and civil rights activist / Susan Sinnott ; foreword by Thulani Davis.
        p.   cm. (The Barnard Biography series)
Includes bibliographical references (p. 135) and index.
SUMMARY: Examines the life and work of this African American playwright and social activist who received great recognition at an early age.
        ISBN: 1-57324-093-1
        1. Hansberry, Lorraine, 1930–1965—Juvenile literature. 2. Women dramatists, American—20th century—Biography—Juvenile literature. 3. Afro-American women civil rights workers—Biography—Juvenile literature. 4. Afro-American dramatists—Biography—Juvenile literature. 5. Afro-Americans in literature—Juvenile literature.
[1. Hansberry, Lorraine, 1930–1965. 2.Dramatists, American. 3. Civil rights workers. 4. Afro-Americans—Biography. 5. Women—Biography.]
I. Title. II. Series: Barnard biography series (Berkeley, Calif.)
        PS3515.A515 Z875   1999
        812'.54—dc21
        [B]   98–50507
                                                                        CIP
                                                                         AC

Photographs courtesy of AP Wide World Photos, Corbis-Bettman, and the Estate of Robert Nemiroff.

Selections from *Collected Poems* by Langston Hughes, Copyright © 1994 by the Estate of Langston Hughes. Reprinted by permission of Alfred A Knopf Inc.

Printed in the United States of America on recycled paper

        99   00   01   02   03   DR   1   2   3   4   5 6   7 8   9   10

To my wonderful friend and
South Side tour guide,
Charnan Simon

Lorraine Hansberry

Foreword

In 1959, when Lorraine Hansberry's play *A Raisin in the Sun* opened on Broadway, the world I knew was still rather flat. Her very existence as a brilliant writer, "black and a female," as she said, was considered an absolute rarity. African American women writers were a hidden treasure, apt to be discovered only when a caring teacher or parent gave one of their books to a young reader. In some ways this is still true, but Lorraine Hansberry became such a phenomenon at the age of twenty-nine, so young, so brilliant, so marvelously articulate, that she cleared a space in American theater for new voices. But more importantly, she showed many of us with young and as yet unformed minds how to follow our gifts and go where they take us.

The works of African American women writers were rarely taught outside the all-black schools within the segregated South, where young people like me learned black writers by heart, and carried them in our minds instead of our textbooks. Then, at the onset of the sixties, an era of enormous social change in America, Lorraine Hansberry represented many of these unknown voices as her fame spread across the country.

When *A Raisin in the Sun* opened on Broadway, it became the most notable play in America by a black playwright, and today, thirty-five years later, it still can be said to hold that place. Hansberry was the youngest playwright, and the first black, to win the New York Drama Critics' Circle Award for Best Play of the Year. Americans discovered this young woman in photo spreads in *Life* magazine and on television, and we African Americans heard her giving *our* message, our poetry, to the world.

As I got older, and began to study and read more of her other work, I found in her not only inspiration, but also ideas that needed to be followed and developed. Because she died so young, many people did not get to know the great breadth of her work: her other plays, which were not all produced in her short life; articles she wrote as a journalist; speeches she made around the country; and a novel she worked on until her death. But looking at the work now, I can say that she was quite ahead of her time, and, in fact, led the way for many writers who came along later in the sixties and seventies.

Hansberry was committed to the idea that a writer's work must deal with the social and political realities of its time. "The question is not whether one will make a social statement in one's work—but only what the statement will say, for if it says anything at all, it will be social," she said. She wanted to focus our attention on the problems of race in America, and the many complicated and conflicting ideas people have about how everyone else in America should conform to their personal beliefs. But she also said that race is only one vehicle people use to exert power over other people.

LORRAINE HANSBERRY

In *A Raisin in the Sun,* Hansberry shows us that we all struggle with our own individual dreams, even while we try to work for a common good. Within a black family that moves to a new house in an all-white neighborhood, in an effort to better their lives, there is not just one idea of freedom but many, and yet there is a common good, a way for each to help and all to help. Lena Younger, the mother, dreams of moving her family to a home more hospitable than their Chicago tenement. Her son Walter Jr. dreams of giving up his chauffeur's job to build his own business, but in trying to do that, he loses part of the family's small legacy. Beneatha Younger, Lena's daughter, a college student hoping to go to medical school, sees her dream threatened by those of the others.

In creating these characters, Hansberry gives us a carefully crafted view of what manhood is for many blacks, what womanhood means, and how men and women define themselves as human beings. And the play helps us to discover how much stronger we can become by learning to make room even for the mistakes of those who dream around us, and how, often, the dream of another, a loved one or someone who came before us, can give us the muscle we need.

Hansberry created women characters who were well aware of the ways in which women are often forced to forego their dreams for the sake of others, and how little is expected of them as they go through life. And she wrote about the problems we have in seeing those around us who do not live as well as us or share our opportunities, those considered outsiders for any number of reasons.

Hansberry was the first American playwright to get us

to think about the connections between Africa and America, Africa and African Americans. In *A Raisin in the Sun*, she begins to use what she was learning about African history and politics and, in this play, was one of the first writers to anticipate the passion for discovering "roots" and all things African that would sweep black communities in the sixties. In the play *Les Blancs*, she wrote about the sometimes bloody struggle Africans waged in the sixties for independence from Europe, and how those important battles often set brother against brother, just as the Civil War left the American family divided. The scenes she set in Chicago or West Africa, New York or South Africa still play out today, on many stages, and in our lives.

Before her death, Lorraine Hansberry also worked on a novel, which still has not been published. *All the Dark and Beautiful Warriors* is based on some of her own life experiences as a middle-class girl in Chicago and as a student at the University of Wisconsin. It tells the story of a bright, exuberant, and intellectually curious young black woman and her desire to overcome the ways in which her life at home sheltered her from the rest of the world, particularly from the day-to-day work of the civil rights movement then taking shape in America. In this book, she explored even further all that she was learning about the issues with which Africans were struggling. Some of those issues have only come into discussion in mainstream America in the last few years. Had she been able to finish the book and publish it in the mid-sixties, no doubt it would have been a groundbreaking work and be known today as the first of a boom of important novels by African American women.

But even without this last gift from Lorraine Hansberry, we are very rich for having the works she did publish. Her presence among us is still almost magical. She continues to inspire and to raise questions the rest of us must try to answer. Hansberry infused a generation of writers, not only playwrights but poets and novelists as well, with her passionate vision. A writer who leaves us with a sense that we must continue her journey, who sends us packing with our dreams and questions, is a great writer indeed. She could do no more.

Thulani Davis

ONE

A Sweet Promise

It has become a sweet promise, hiding, whispering
to me daily ... fame! I shock myself with such
thoughts and shake my head with embarrassment
... fame!

—Lorraine Hansberry,
To Be Young, Gifted, and Black

LORRAINE HANSBERRY, twenty-eight years old, was back
in Chicago, and she was about to become a star.
Everyone around her could feel it; she could, too. Her
play *A Raisin in the Sun* was scheduled for a brief run at
the Blackstone Theater and would then move to
Broadway in early March. Its success was, as one reporter
wrote, the story of an "emerging bombshell." Not only
did everyone want to interview Lorraine, they seemed to
crave her opinion on everything—theater, life, and, most
of all, what it was like to be black in America in 1959.

So Lorraine was almost relieved when she walked into
her mother's house on South Park Way and her older sister

Mamie immediately began to complain about Lorraine's sloppy clothes and careless grooming. "Just like old times," Lorraine thought. She only shrugged, mumbling something to Mamie about not having had much time to think about her clothes, what with all the rehearsals, tryouts in New Haven and Philadelphia, meetings, and late nights. She hoped Mamie would take the hint and drop the subject.

"This is Chicago!" Mamie threw her hands up in despair. "You're not really going on to the stage in blue jeans!" she exclaimed, and then begged Lorraine to let her pick out a new dress for the opening. She knew just where to go to find something really chic. The family didn't want her to embarrass them, after all.

Yet Lorraine hardly needed to be reminded of where she was. Didn't her own nerves, wound much more tightly now than at any time during the last six weeks, tell her that? *A Raisin in the Sun,* after all, was set in Chicago. It was *about* Chicago, at least a certain part of it—the South Side's so-called Black Metropolis, where the Hansberry family still lived. It was also about a certain family, the Youngers, who were poor and working class, and had only a flickering hope that life could match their dreams.

Lorraine Hansberry had spent her entire Chicago childhood looking into the lives of her South Side neighbors, people just like the Youngers. She'd listened to little boys talk tough and watched them shadowbox like their idol, Joe Louis. She'd stood close by while skinny-legged girls jumped double dutch to rousing singsongs that made them go faster and faster. How Lorraine had envied the neighborhood kids their independence, brashness, even the violence that was part of their daily lives!

She had rarely been asked to join in the games, though; she couldn't get the steps or the words just right. *She'd been different.* She'd been a girl whose father had scratched out the word "Negro" on her official State of Illinois birth certificate and written in "black" instead. "Black must mean that I'm different," she thought, when she was old enough to hear about how Carl had changed the birth certificate, but still too young to understand its meaning. *Black and proud and different.* So she'd stood by and watched, as though her nose were pressed hard against a windowpane.

People like the Youngers didn't try to hide the shabbiness that was everywhere around them. Porches sagged, unpainted steps split and broke apart. Full clotheslines waved in the dirty Chicago wind. As Lorraine saw it, their segregated lives were a form of protest, the sooty clothing their banners.

Yes, here in Chicago, everything would be much more personal. The audiences would be full of people who had known her as a shy, chubby, serious-talking young girl. There would be many, too, who remembered her father Carl Hansberry, a successful real estate broker. Carl had devoted years of his life to challenging the city's restrictive housing laws and, more than twenty years earlier, had enlisted his whole family in the battle.

In the summer of 1938, the Hansberrys had bought a home in Chicago's all-white Washington Park neighborhood, which bordered the University of Chicago. It had been, as Lorraine remembered it, a "hellishly hostile" place. One day soon after moving in, she and Mamie sat on their front porch, passing the afternoon on a hanging swing. Suddenly, a large, angry crowd gathered. The two sisters ran inside the house and, as they stood in the living room with their mother, someone hurled a brick through the front window with such force that it lodged in the plaster wall. It had missed Lorraine's head by less than an inch.

By the end of that summer, the Hansberry family had been given a court order to leave the neighborhood. Carl, along with the National Association for the Advancement of Colored People (NAACP), filed suit. They took the case, *Hansberry v. Lee,* all the way to the Supreme Court and won in 1940. Within a few years, however, as Carl faced the realization that changing laws and changing attitudes are two different struggles, the victory became hollow. Before he died in 1946, Carl became discouraged and disillusioned, uncertain if there was such a thing as justice for the black man in America.

Reporters always seemed to want to know the whys and hows of *A Raisin in the Sun,* and Lorraine scarcely knew what to say. Should she talk about her own father and mother, and their tremendous persistence and courage? Or, should she talk about the time she was an eighteen-year-old college student who walked into the rehearsal of a student production of *Juno and the Paycock* at the University of Wisconsin Theater? As soon as she heard playwright Sean O'Casey's rich dialogue, his exquisite melody, she knew that she, too, would try to write her own melody one day, but "as I knew it—in a different key."

In truth, though, she hadn't thought much about the whys, hadn't separated out the momentous events from the trivial. "Wasn't that for biographers and critics?" she thought, laughing at her own pretentiousness. All she knew was that after years of letting the story slosh about in her head, she had just started in and written it. For eight months in 1956 and 1957, she sat in the little study off the kitchen of her Greenwich Village apartment and typed. She slept little, smoked countless cigarettes, and drank pots of coffee.

There had been many, many times she thought she wouldn't be able to finish. Once, in an explosion of desperation, she tossed the entire manuscript high in the air and stomped out of the room. Bob—her husband, Robert Nemiroff—had gotten down on the floor, picked up each page, and put them all back in order. Then he put the play in a box and hid it for several days, until he thought Lorraine could face her work once again.

When she did, it came easily. The dialogue seemed to flow from the typewriter onto the paper. Then, when she finished typing, ripped the last page from the carriage, and placed it carefully at the bottom of the manuscript, she lay face down on her living room carpet and stretched her hands and feet as far as they could go. She had done it—she had written her play! It was no longer inside her; it was there in that pile. It was a lovely little bundle that she could now wrap in a neat package and send out to the world. As she wrote to her mother from her hotel room in New Haven, Connecticut, just before *A Raisin in the Sun*'s first preview performance in January 1959:

Mama, it is a play that tells the truth about people. Negroes and life and I think it will help a lot of people to understand how we are just as complicated as they are—

5

and just as mixed up—but above all, that we have among our miserable and downtrodden ranks people who are the very essence of human dignity. That is what, after all the laughter and tears, the play is supposed to say. I hope it will make you very proud. . . .

Now, a few weeks later, as she waited for the opening night in Chicago, she felt like a nervous parent watching her only child grow up and strike out on its own. During rehearsals, sitting about ten rows back from the stage, she marveled at the set. The Youngers' apartment was a perfect replica of a Chicago-style kitchenette, just like in the kinds of places her father had rented out over and over again during the Depression. She could admire, too, the stunning cast—which included the magnetic, powerful Sidney Poitier, Ruby Dee, and Claudia McNeil—who breathed vibrant life into her paper characters. How had it happened that in America—which in 1959 was only just considering full racial integration—an unknown black playwright and director and a distinguished, though still little-known, group of actors stood poised and ready to capture the heart and soul of Broadway? How was it that she, Lorraine Hansberry, was at the center of this swirl?

In the end, Lorraine gave her sister Mamie permission to buy her something black and elegant at one of Michigan Avenue's smart dress shops. She only asked that Mamie forgive her if she really couldn't concentrate on that sort of thing, not now, not with this noise constantly in her head. What was it? It was a kind of buzzing that she'd first heard very faintly that first week in New Haven back in January. Now it was getting louder, almost drowning out everything else. Was it really the sound of

an emerging bombshell, or was it, as another reporter offered, that Goddess Success? Or was it fame . . . just fame?
All Lorraine knew was that, whatever it was, it was coming closer, about to turn her life upside-down. And it was
too late to get out of the way, even if she wanted to. . . .

TWO

Chicago

> I was born on the Southside of Chicago. I was born
> black and a female. I was born in a depression after
> one world war and came into my adolescence dur-
> ing another. . . .
>
> —Lorraine Hansberry,
> *To Be Young, Gifted, and Black*

L ORRAINE'S OWN PARENTS, Carl and Nannie Hansberry,
seemed born to a life of genteel protest. They were
considered educated and refined by their community
and, above all, they were *proud* people, proud of their
country and their race. When Lorraine was born, on May
19, 1930, Carl and Nannie were both active members of
the National Association for the Advancement of Colored
People (NAACP), the Chicago Urban League, *and* the
Republican Party. Carl didn't see any contradiction in
these various affiliations. His lifelong goal was to give
blacks the freedom to become just as rich and powerful as
any white man—especially those who were bent on deny-
ing men like Carl any opportunity at all.

Carl August Hansberry was born in Gloster, Missississippi, in 1895. His grandfather William Hansberry had been born a slave in Culpepper County, Virginia. William's mother was African, and his father was the plantation's master. That fact, however, didn't prevent him from selling his son "down the river"—to harsher conditions in Louisiana—when William was fifteen.

William Hansberry was more fortunate than most slaves sent to the Deep South, however. His new master, Mr. Young, valued William's craftsmanship and treated him fairly and humanely. By 1864, with the South's defeat in the Civil War all but certain, Mr. Young asked William to help him hide the family's gold, silver, and jewelry in a nearby woods. Together, they dug several holes and buried everything. Before the war ended, however, Mr. Young was killed as he tried to cross Union lines. William later retrieved the treasure and over several years invested it carefully and cautiously, in both land and education for his family of ten children. One of his sons, Mender Hansberry, attended Alcorn College and married a fellow student, Ethel Frances Woodward. They both became teachers and raised their six children, including Carl Hansberry, in Gloster, Mississippi.

Carl, too, attended Alcorn College, the "family school." But by the time he graduated in 1915, blacks were leaving the South by the thousands, boarding trains for the great northern industrial centers, captivated by the "promise of the North." These trains followed the routes of the Underground Railroad which fifty years earlier had led thousands north, out of slavery. Then, before the Civil War, terrified slaves had fled their quarters at night, running across open fields and into the nearest woods. Now—nearly two generations since slavery's end in 1863—blacks stood in broad daylight on the platform of train stations in cities like Biloxi, Mississippi, and Macon, Georgia, carrying their few belongings in cardboard suitcases tied together with string. Their destinations were often a matter of train connections: From Virginia and the Carolinas, migrants went to Baltimore, Philadelphia, or New York City. From parts of Alabama, Georgia, and Kentucky, they headed for Pittsburgh or Cleveland. And those from Mississippi, Arkansas, Tennessee, or Louisiana rode the Illinois Central Railroad to Chicago.

Carl Hansberry, whose background and education separated him from many of his fellow migrants, was linked to them by the belief that there was no future for the colored man in the Deep South. There had been a brief period just after the Civil War when one could have hoped it would be otherwise. Carl Hansberry's grandparents might have felt it in Mississippi during the late 1860s, but such optimism didn't last long. Ultimately, Southern tradition—what the esteemed black author and educator W. E. B. DuBois called a "system of caste and insult"—dictated that blacks and whites would never be treated equally in any sphere of society.

The infamous Jim Crow laws, first enacted in 1877, made DuBois' words a reality. Jim Crow was the name of a well-known character in minstrel shows, which featured white entertainers wearing black makeup and acting out a stereotype of the slow-witted slave. This crow's antics were intentionally offensive and his name—always despised by black people—soon became synonymous with segregation. Sharecrop farming—destined to be Carl Hansberry's life unless he finished school—was nothing more than the Jim Crow South's form of legalized slavery.

So in 1914, when word spread that jobs were plentiful in such northern industrial cities as Chicago, St. Louis, and New York, there was more than a buzz of interest. The great war just beginning in Europe had completely cut off the flow of immigrant workers from the countries of Eastern and Central Europe, and suddenly the steel mills, meat-packing plants, and railroad yards were calling for help. Chicago-based companies like Armour, Swift, and McCormack turned to the untapped supply of labor in the South to fill these high-wage jobs. At first "the word" was just a whisper, passed from train porters to southbound passengers and on to rural townspeople. But soon talk of well-paying jobs up north was on just about everyone's lips. *I pick up my life and take it away,* Langston Hughes wrote in his poem "One-Way Ticket": *On a one-way ticket/Gone up North, Gone out West, Gone!*

There were other northern destinations, of course, but Chicago was special. A frontier outpost only a couple of generations earlier, it now seemed the very place to lead the world into the twentieth century. Black people knew it as not only the home of the Sears catalog but as a city that supported such black-owned enterprises as Provident Hospital, two banks, and even a professional baseball team. And it was where the flamboyant Robert Sengstacke Abbott published the straight-talking newspaper, the *Daily Defender.*

Abbott, born in rural Georgia, first traveled to Chicago to perform at the 1893 World's Columbian Exposition with a vocal quartet from the Hampton Institute. He was captivated by the gritty, fast-moving city and returned in 1897, hoping to become a journalist. Unable to find a newspaper job, however, he enrolled in law school. After a prominent attorney informed him he was "too dark" to ever be taken seriously in a courtroom, Robert Abbott hatched another plan. In 1905, he printed a few copies of "The World's Greatest Weekly," as the *Defender* boldly called itself, and then he sold them on the street corner. He built his newspaper empire both by extolling the glories of big, burly Chicago and by telling the South's *real* story—the one blacks were too fearful to tell themselves. The *Defender* had the boldness to speak loudly—and luridly—about lynchings, mob violence, and the many degradations of daily life. "WHEN THE MOB COMES AND YOU MUST DIE TAKE AT LEAST ONE WITH YOU," shouted one headline.

For Southern blacks, who comprised more than half of the *Defender*'s readers, this combination of pride, dignity, and assertiveness represented all that was missing in their own lives. In Mississippi, a man could be lynched for merely brushing against a white woman while he ran for a train. In Chicago, "God's Country," it was said you could go anywhere, anytime. Why, the *Defender* even reported that prizefighter Jack Johnson rode right down Michigan Avenue in a big, shiny car with a white woman at his side!

Carl Hansberry's dreams, on the other hand, were strictly middle class. He wanted to own a home in a decent neighborhood, give his children a good education, and provide material comforts for his entire family. In 1915, however, a black man could be considered a dewy-eyed optimist for thinking such dreams would ever come true. Bright, ambitious, and very determined, Carl soon took a job with the fledgling Binga Bank, one of the city's two black-owned banks. At the nearby Lake Street Bank, Carl met a pretty young teller named Nannie Perry.

Nannie's background was similar to Carl's. Her father, George Perry, had been born a slave, though he'd escaped from his master's Tennessee plantation when he was only twelve and fled to New York City. There he worked for a theater company and hired a tutor to teach him to read and write. Within a few years, George returned to Tennessee and paid his master for his and his mother's freedom. He eventually married a half-black, half-Cherokee woman named Charlotte Organ and settled in Columbia, Tennessee, where he became a minister in the African Methodist Episcopal Church. Self-improvement through education was every bit as important to the Perry family as it had been among the Hansberrys. George insisted his that six children go to school for as long as they could. His daughter Nannie attended Tennessee Agricultural University—something that was very unusual for a black woman at the beginning of the twentieth century—before deciding to seek a better life in Chicago. She and Carl Hansberry were married in 1916, a year after they'd first met.

Despite being part of Chicago's black "business class," the Hansberrys' first home was one room in a shabby South Side tenement building. When Carl Jr. was born the following year, they moved again, this time into a one-bedroom apartment. When their second child Perry was born in 1919, they moved once more. Each time they changed residences, however, their living conditions improved only slightly. Rents were extremely high, and the only apartments available to them were within the boundaries of Bronzeville, as the South Side was also known. Carl chafed at the reality of the situation: despite his and Nannie's relative wealth and prosperity, they were trapped in the ghetto.

The sad fact was that Chicago's heart did not seem able to stretch to include the nearly 200,000 mostly uneducated blacks who had streamed in from the South since the start of World War I. When it became clear that blacks intended to live side by side with whites, and as equals, the reaction of white Chicago was grimly predictable. Just like their Southern brethren, they resorted to discrimination and segregation. Since, however, such overt practices were against the law in the North, whites looked for subtle legal means to keep blacks separate.

One of these was the restrictive covenant, which became the principal device for controlling black expansion into white, usually middle-class, neighborhoods. This covenant might be nothing more than a sentence or two in the property's deed, which stated that the house or apartment could not be sold or rented to blacks. Even though the constitutionality of such agreements was very doubtful, they were routinely upheld by judges and used by landlords and real estate developers alike. By 1920, three-quarters of Chicago's real estate was "protected" by restrictive covenants. The result was that blacks, even those who would have been able to afford much better housing in nearby neighborhoods, were unable to move from the segregated Black Belt.

The conditions created by the combination of an aged and dwindling supply of housing and ever-growing numbers of migrants arriving from the South were alarming. Broken-down tenements, often with boarded windows, leaned precariously against one another. Empty lots, squeezed in between rows of wooden houses, were filled with rubble and piles of garbage. The tension created by overcrowding and squalor turned violent when, at the end of World War I, returning soldiers forced black workers out of the jobs that had brought them north in the first place—and which were their only source of hope and pride.

When, in July 1919, a black boy mistakenly walked onto an all-white segregated Lake Michigan beach and was killed, racial animosity could no longer be contained. For five days, assaults and random shootings left the streets of Chicago in a state of siege. When the riots were over, twenty-three blacks and fifteen whites were dead, thousands injured, and countless South Side businesses and residences destroyed. The rage and violence of Red Summer, as it became known, shocked everyone, and forced city leaders to look hard for paths of reconciliation.

Red Summer changed the course of Carl Hansberry's life. He felt, as the poet Claude McKay wrote that summer in "If We Must Die," that *Like men we'll face the murderous cowardly pack/Pressed to the wall, dying, but fighting back!* Carl realized blacks like him would need to do more for their own community than simply set an example by hard work and material prosperity. He and Nannie both became dedicated activists, first by increasing their commitment to the NAACP. Carl also joined the newly formed Chicago Urban League, a branch of the National League on Urban Conditions (later called the National Urban League) whose mission was to alleviate the acute housing crisis and help the rural poor adjust to modern life in the city.

By the time the Hansberrys' first daughter Mamie was born in 1922, Carl had become the head of his own small company, which had begun to buy houses and apartment buildings throughout the South Side. He also attempted several times to move his family into one of the middle-class neighborhoods that abutted Bronzeville, each time being beaten back by restrictive covenant statutes. Thoroughly frustrated by the gross injustice of these so-called laws, he undertook a series of challenges, all with the support of the NAACP. As Carl won some small victories, he gained a reputation as a hard-nosed and aggressive fighter for equal access to housing.

When the Great Depression began in late 1929, Carl Hansberry lost many of his real estate holdings. Yet Carl, who was serving a two-year term as U.S. Deputy Marshall, to which he'd been appointed by President Herbert Hoover, did not panic. He simply started over. Hansberry Enterprises, a "Rooming House Business," seemed to rise miraculously from ruin, and even prospered during the Depression, a fact that embarrassed the Hansberrys' youngest child Lorraine, when she was old enough to realize the secret behind the success that separated her from her South Side neighbors: the infamous kitchenette apartment. In order to meet the huge demand for more living space, Carl began converting many of his buildings into smaller units—and thus earned the controversial nickname the "kitchenette king."

While such apartments did provide living space for needy families, the overcrowding that resulted strained living conditions even further. Kitchenettes—like the Youngers' apartment in *A Raisin in the Sun*—were created by taking, for example, a six-room apartment and converting it to six one-room households. The kitchenette would include a hot plate, ice box, and a bed; the one bathroom would be in the main hall and shared by all six families. St. Clair Drake and Horace R. Cayton, authors of *Black Metropolis,* the landmark study of Chicago's South Side, described kitchenettes as a menace to both health and morals. Richard Wright's influential novel *Native Son* also focused attention on the tragic consequences of such overcrowding. Wright's main character, a young Chicago black named Bigger Thomas, is unable to withstand the crushing psychological pressures of slum life.

Still, Hansberry Enterprises insisted their intention was not just profit, but that they were able to help people who had no other housing available. If they prospered during the Depression, the company maintained, it was because they took care of their properties and could collect rents when many white landlords couldn't. Lorraine's own ambivalence about her father's business can be found at the very core of *A Raisin in the Sun.*

All Lorraine remembered of those early years, however, is how often her father was away from home and how much she missed him. She grew to resent that her parents' passion for social causes kept them distant from their children, especially their youngest one. As Lorraine observed with some bitterness, "Of love and my parents there is little to be written. . . . We were fed and housed and dressed and outfitted with more cash than our associates and that was all. . . ."

As she watched her father bustle to his office, or to Washington and New York, Lorraine imagined he was always doing something brilliant and important. If the Hansberrys had guests for Sunday dinner, they would include the most celebrated blacks of the day, people like composer and band leader Duke Ellington, W. E. B. DuBois, Langston Hughes, or singer and activist Paul Robeson. To Lorraine, Carl Hansberry seemed larger than life and afraid of absolutely nothing. Which is why it was so disturbing when she learned that not only did he know fear but, just like his South Side neighbors, he could be crushed by disappointment.

THREE

Little Girl in White Fur

Above all, there had been an aspect of the society
of kids from the ghetto which demanded utmost
respect: they fought. The girls as well as the boys.
THEY FOUGHT.

—Lorraine Hansberry,
To Be Young, Gifted, and Black

LORRAINE HAD FIRST NOTICED the big, glimmery box
under the tree days before Christmas. It was by far the
largest present, and its wrapping paper was as shiny as
the tinsel hanging from the pine branches. When sister
Mamie told Lorraine the present was for her, Lorraine
couldn't believe her luck. At five, years younger than
Mamie, or Perry, or Carl Jr., Lorraine was considered the
silly little clown of the family, her sister's and brothers'
toy. How did it happen, then, that she was to receive the
best present that year? Her excitement grew as she
counted off the long days that remained until Christmas.

When Christmas morning arrived and it was finally

time to open the cherished gift, Lorraine's family closed in around her to watch every nuance of her reaction. Only there weren't any nuances; there was only outrage. Her mouth turned down and tears gathered in her eyes. No one noticed, though. They screeched in excitement as Lorraine lifted the white rabbit fur coat from its tissue-paper nest and then clapped gleefully as Mother draped it over her limp shoulders. Next came the matching cap and muff, and then Lorraine was coaxed to walk down the hall so she could see herself in the full-length mirror. She looked, she later recalled, like one of those big stupid rabbits in her coloring books. And she *hated* those rabbits.

Lorraine insisted she wouldn't wear her new outfit to school, but her mother would have none of it. *You must, dear. . . . We're so proud!* And so, Lorraine walked up the steps of Betsy Ross Elementary on the next school day, dressed entirely in white fur. It was the beginning of 1936, the heart of the Great Depression. She knew that her classmates came to school hungry, wearing thread-bare sweaters and light jackets that barely protected them from Chicago's fierce winter winds. She knew what they were going to think of her fancy new Christmas clothes— and what they would do. Almost as soon as she crossed the sidewalk to the schoolyard, they set upon her, hitting her with their fists and pouring ink all over the white fur.

The odd thing was, as Lorraine remembered, she respected those kids for their reaction. They seemed like grownups, she thought, with their ability to fight back, their fierce independence, their street-smarts. They had *authority*. She, on the other hand, was her family's pet, dressed like a princess to show off their wealth. She despised herself for being so gawky and pampered and *different*.

A few years later, when Lorraine first noticed that these same kids wore gleaming house keys on strings around their necks, she longed for the same token of independence. She wanted the world to think she, too, was on her own, coming and going when she pleased, answering to no one. In an act of defiant solidarity, she tied her roller skate key around her neck and wore it for days. It wasn't the same, though. Nothing different happened, and her brothers, of course, just laughed and laughed.

Lorraine blamed her parents for everything that separated her from her classmates. They were the ones who chose the Jim Crow schools on the South Side, where the teachers were poorly trained, the school day lasted only three hours, and the buildings were designed to be inferior. "I was given during the grade school years one half the amount of education prescribed for each child by the Board of Education of my city," she told a gathering of magazine editors late in her life. "This was so because the children of the Chicago ghetto were jammed into a segregated school system. To this day, I do not add, subtract, or multiply with ease."

The Hansberrys could afford private schools, which their friends' children attended, but they chose public as a way of showing support for the black community. At Betsy Ross Elementary and, in the later grades, at A. O. Sexton, Lorraine was a star in arithmetic as well as reading and writing. Only later did she realize that, compared to white public-school students, she could scarcely count or do the most basic calculations.

Since Carl Hansberry was gone most of the time—at his office or meeting with someone important—Lorraine heaped most of her disdain and frustration on her mother, whose refined ways seemed to be at the root of her problem. Nannie Hansberry was, Lorraine believed, entirely too formal and too perfect. She always appeared in the family's carpeted living room dressed to go out— her seamed stockings perfectly straight, high heels, purse, and hat all perfectly coordinated. "Vain and intensely feminine," is how Nannie's youngest daughter once described her, adding sarcastically that she was a true daughter of the South. She wasn't at all like the mother of Lorraine's friend Carmen Smith, who lay on a bare mattress on the floor, too tired or sick to get up. Carmen made her own bologna sandwiches on squishy white bread and, of course, let herself in and out of the apartment with her very own key.

What Lorraine didn't, or couldn't have, understood about her mother at the time was that Nannie was raised as a proud fighter. Her banner was not only that of the Negro race, as Nannie's generation called themselves, but the middle class as well, the right to *be* middle class. Nannie never forgot that her father had been born into slavery. He'd talked little of that "peculiar institution," but made it clear to each of his children that the climb out of such an extreme humiliation was ever upward. There was no turning back.

Sometimes, on hot Chicago summer nights, the Hansberry family would leave their sweltering apartment, drive to a park along Lake Michigan, and spread out a blanket. Lorraine remembered that Carl would lie on his back, stare up at the constellations, and tell them stories. Her favorite tale was about slaves escaping north by following the Big Dipper—the Drinking Gourd, as they called it—which pointed toward the North Star. Her father seemed to know everything about the stars, yet most of the time Lorraine scarcely even noticed them in the bright big-city sky.

During the summer of 1938, Lorraine began to appreciate the forces that molded her parents, when her family attempted to move into a new house in the Washington Park neighborhood, a "white island" in the middle of the South Side's black belt. Carl agreed to buy the property as part of an NAACP strategy to test Chicago's discriminatory housing laws. He received help in purchasing the property from a white insurance executive and several white realtors who, for their own business reasons, believed the time had come to end racially based covenants. With their help, Carl bought the property on Rhodes Avenue without revealing his real name or the fact that he was black. As soon as the "secret" was out, however, a woman named Anna M. Lee filed suit against Carl on behalf of the Woodlawn Property Owners' Association, which represented nearly 500 white residents. The Circuit Court of Cook County quickly sided with Lee and ordered Carl to give up the property. Carl and the NAACP immediately appealed, and the Hansberry family prepared to move into their house.

That summer, Lorraine saw a very different side of her mother, one she couldn't help but respect. The legal proceeding took Carl to Illinois' capitol, Springfield, for long stretches, and so Nannie and the children faced the angry neighbors—the "howling mobs," as Lorraine described them—alone. It was a very scary and dangerous time, and Lorraine was amazed at her mother's cool-headed courage. Weeks after the cement brick crashed through the living room window, Nannie still stayed up all night, patrolling the house with a loaded pistol in her hand.

Later that same summer, Nannie Hansberry, her sister, and a gang of cousins piled into the family's black Cadillac and drove to Tennessee to visit Grandma Perry. It was a welcome break from the tense Chicago summer. Lorraine never forgot the long, lazy drive and how the flat Illinois farmland turned to soft rolling hills in a place called Kentucky. As the gentle pastures became the tree-covered rounded hills of Tennessee, Nannie began to chatter happily about her own parents and grandparents. She talked about her father, who had been born on a plantation near Columbia, Tennessee, and who had often snuck off into the very same hills when he was only seven or eight. His frantic mother—Lorraine's great-grandmother—had risked her own safety, heading into the hills by moonlight to leave food for him.

By the time the Cadillac turned down the dirt road and approached the small rough-hewn cabin, Lorraine could hardly wait to meet her grandmother, who'd always been described as a great beauty. When she finally caught sight of the tiny wrinkled woman sitting in a cane rocker, however, she wondered how *this* could be her lovely grandmother. This woman could barely see or hear, and her mind seemed to be in a faraway place. Lorraine struggled to overcome her disappointment and anger, speaking only a little at first.

Later though, as the family gathered on the porch in the hot Tennessee night, eating cornmeal cupcakes and drinking sweet lemonade, Grandmother Perry began to tell stories of her past. She talked about slaves and slave-owners, too, and about something or someone called a "master." Lorraine turned everything over and over in her mind, trying to make sense of so much unsettling history. A master, it seemed from what all the adults said, had absolute control over both life and death. A slave was the master's property, like a plow or a mule.

The next morning, Lorraine convinced her younger cousin Shauneille to walk with her far into the wooded hills behind the cabin. They were to go alone, Lorraine explained, without telling anyone—it was all part of the game. Shauneille hesitated at first, but Lorraine insisted everything would be all right. They were to pretend they were runaway slaves, trying to evade the master and his vicious hounds.

The cousins stayed out all day. They ran through the woods, holding fast to brush and seedlings so they wouldn't be caught by the master. When they finally returned to the cabin, late in the afternoon, their mothers were furious with them for not telling anyone they were leaving, and for being gone so long. As Shauneille sobbed uncontrollably, Lorraine accepted full blame for planning the escape. "Lorraine got a spanking but didn't cry," Shauneille remembered years later. And she scolded Shauneille, who was not punished, for showing so much emotion. Hadn't Shauneille understood that the game hadn't ended when they left the woods? That maybe the game would never end? The most important part was one's will to resist. Lorraine went to bed happy that night, knowing that out of her whole family, she would have been the most defiant slave of all.

Back in Chicago, the Hansberrys withstood the hostility of their white neighbors for several more months. Finally, late in 1938, Carl Hansberry and the NAACP lost their bid to have the Cook County Circuit Court decision reversed by the Illinois Supreme Court. Even though the lawyers decided to appeal the decision to the United States Supreme Court, the family was evicted from the Rhodes Avenue home in what seemed like a victory for the racist neighbors. Despite the legal setback, eight-year-old Lorraine remembered leaving Washington Park with some relief. The family moved into a fine brick home on South Park Way, one of the South Side's main thoroughfares.

As the 1930s came to a close, Lorraine felt herself hurtling toward adolescence without much grace or confidence. Her weight ballooned and she had to bear the jeers of her classmates. At home, her family seemed to think of her only as a chubby little clown. Out in the world, where she was quiet and painfully shy, she was considered a loner who preferred the company of books to that of her peers.

It was at this time that she first read the work of one of her father's friends, the poet Langston Hughes, who visited the Hansberry house whenever he was in Chicago. Ever since she was a little girl, Lorraine had thought of Mr. Hughes as one of the kindest of their visitors. After spending some time talking to Carl in his study, he would come into the living room, clasp Lorraine's hand, and tell her just how much he'd enjoyed his visit. Not until Lorraine was ten years old, however, did she begin to understand exactly who this friendly man really was: He was the poet of the Jazz Age and the Harlem Renaissance, as well as the voice of the "everyday" black person.

Lorraine loved to slip into her father's study, pull down Mr. Hughes' books of poetry from the shelf, and let the melody of his words flow over her. How had he done it? How had he made these lowly black folk sing so tunefully? As she began to write her own poems and sketches, she longed to do the same thing, to bring ordinary people—the very ones who had lived in her father's kitchenette apartments—to wonderful, vivid life. *If I can give these people a voice*, she thought, *others might know and care about them, and then the ghosts of their masters might finally be laid to rest.*

The Book of

Lorraine Hansberry

A Review of a Year,
January, 1947, to January, 1948.

ENGLEWOOD HIGH SCHOOL
CHICAGO, ILLINOIS

LORRAINE VIVIAN HANSBERRY
President, Forum
Gym secretary
To be a journalist

FOUR

Coming of Age

I tire so of hearing people say,
Let things take their course.
Tomorrow is another day.
I do not need freedom when I'm dead.
I cannot live on tomorrow's bread.

—Langston Hughes, in *Freedom*

L ORRAINE WASN'T like her older sister Mamie. Mamie was pretty, vivacious, and extremely popular; Lorraine was none of these. Instead, she was an outsider, the one who watched the others from a distance but didn't join in. She liked to spend long hours in her room reading, drawing, and writing poems. When Lorraine turned fourteen, it often seemed that all she would ever know of boyfriends, football games, and school dances would come from quizzing the college boys who waited up to thirty minutes in the Hansberry living room while Mamie finished applying her makeup.

One September evening, a nice young man called for Mamie. Lorraine recognized him as a former Englewood

High football star. While he sat uneasily on the sofa, Lorraine settled into a stuffed armchair just across from him. She looked at him hard and then, after a few minutes of silence, began asking questions. "What's it like being a football player? What does the roaring crowd sound like from the middle of the playing field?" She knew everyone at Englewood High cared passionately about football, but she had never even been to a game. The young man answered matter of factly, mostly looking at his feet or glancing upward toward Mamie's room, yet Lorraine was captivated. *Football sounded thrilling!*

After Mamie and her date had left, Lorraine went up to her room and began writing. She put down everything the football player had said, filtered through her own imagination. She included the sounds of cheering crowds, the smell of fresh popcorn, the shrill whistle of the referee, and his black-and-white striped shirt against the orange, red, and gold of the autumn afternoon.

First thing that Monday morning, Lorraine gave her story to her English teacher and asked him if he would enter it in the all-school creative writing contest. She didn't tell anyone else what she'd done, not even her own family, so when the principal announced several weeks later that Lorraine Hansberry had won the coveted prize, everyone was stunned. Everyone, that is, except Lorraine. She had set her mind to writing a terrific story, and she had done it. What was so surprising about that?

Entering—and winning—the story contest was only a small sign of Lorraine's new self-confidence. She felt giddy about high school and its many possibilities, not the least of which was interaction, for the first time, with white students. At A. O. Sexton Junior High, she'd been sad and depressed most of the time and never sure why. She knew she had talent and drive—weren't they, after all, the hallmarks of the Hansberry family? But it seemed that the process of polishing the stone, of nurturing her talents, would be a long one and, given her natural shyness and introversion, maybe her gifts would never be shared.

Fortunately for Lorraine, though, she didn't lack role models. Carl and Nannie Hansberry entertained often, and their home on South Park Way had become a Chicago gathering place for the leading black social and literary figures of the day. First there was Carl's brother, William Leo Hansberry, who visited from Washington D.C.'s Howard University, where he was a professor of African Studies. From Uncle Leo, Lorraine learned there was more to Africa than its European colonies. She loved to hear about the Yoruba, Songhay, and Ashanti peoples, and their rich cultural pasts.

There were also memorable visits from W. E. B. DuBois. Dr. DuBois, a founder of the NAACP, author of *The Souls of Black Folk,* and one of the leading black intellectuals and political thinkers of his time, was a great favorite of Carl's. The Hansberrys would host a reception for Dr. DuBois whenever he was in Chicago. While the other guests enjoyed the food, drink, and casual conversation, the two men would slip into Carl's study, light up cigars, and talk about books, ideas, and the state of black people in America.

Among the other famous visitors was Paul Robeson. In 1944, Mr. Robeson was touring the country in a production of Shakespeare's *Othello,* which had run for two years on Broadway. Of course, everyone had heard about Paul Robeson's magnificent voice, his powerful stage presence, and his radical political views. Lorraine found herself speechless when he entered her own living room. She could only stare at him in awe.

Despite the happy buzz of activity at the Hansberry home—the frequent visitors, the marriages of Lorraine's brothers and sister, the arrival of nieces and nephews—the family had grown increasingly concerned about Carl's health. His blood pressure was alarmingly high and he'd become tired and slow. His decline hadn't been sudden, however. Carl had never been the same since the end of 1940, a year of great triumph and crushing disappointment.

Early in that year, the United States Supreme Court ruled in favor of Carl and the NAACP in the case of *Hansberry v. Lee.* This ruling didn't immediately give blacks access to all white-owned property, but it held the promise that similar legal challenges would be ruled in favor of black homeowners. Carl Hansberry, widely praised for his courage and dedication, was considered a hero. By summer he'd decided the time was right for one more uphill battle, this one for a seat in the U.S. House of Representatives. Lorraine, just ten, remembered helping her parents with all the minutiae of political campaigning—stuffing envelopes, going with her father door to door, and passing out leaflets. There was a heady feeling of success in the air, which, unfortunately, did not translate into victory at the polls. Carl was soundly defeated and his hopes for elected office quickly vanished. Afterward it seemed only a cockeyed optimist could have believed that a black Republican with a fervid belief in the free enterprise system would win in an overwhelmingly Democratic district, one that almost exclusively supported President Franklin D. Roosevelt and his New Deal.

A few years later, it was clear to the Hansberry family that Carl had lost more than the election—his fighting spirit was gone, too. By 1941, he realized that even after the long court battle, restrictive covenants were clearly still in place, and that real change would come at an excruciatingly slow pace. The Supreme Court could change laws, it seemed, but not attitudes.

Hansberry Enterprises, too, had suffered during the years of Carl's attention to other matters. Many of his apartment buildings badly needed repair and had begun to lose money. City officials, obviously bitter over Carl's Supreme Court victory, slapped his company with a number of building code violations. Carl took it all very personally. In his own eyes, he seemed to fall from the dizzying heights of success with merciless speed. Lorraine could only see that the man she later described as someone "kings might have imitated" seemed tired, drained, and despondent. He believed he had been wrong about American democracy and about all it could do for the black man. His plight reminded Lorraine of one of Mr. Hughes' poems, which began: *I'm looking for a house/In the world/Where the white shadows/Will not fall,* and ends, despairingly: *There is no such house/Dark brothers/No such house/At all.*

By the end of 1941, the United States had entered World War II and the Hansberrys faced another family crisis. Lorraine's brothers Perry and Carl, Jr. were drafted into the army. Perry, however, stated flatly that he would not serve the United States, since his country had so long denied basic rights to black people. This militant position pitted father against son and added to the family's stress and unhappiness. In the end, both brothers went off to war and returned again in 1945.

Nannie Hansberry tried to protect Lorraine from the family's problems, which suited Lorraine just fine. Like many adolescents, she preferred to be in her room alone with the door shut tight. There she wrote poems, stories—including the one that won the school prize—and furious letters of protest to government officials. She also played jazz and blues records as loudly as she could.

During the summer of 1945, the Hansberrys took a much-anticipated trip to Mexico. They visited good friends, a diplomat and his wife, in the Mexico City suburb of Polanco. Carl loved his stay there and seemed visibly relaxed and healthy. As Mamie remembered, "He said for the first time in his life he felt very free. He felt like a full man." By year's end, Carl and Nannie decided the time had come to leave Hansberry Enterprises in the hands of Carl Jr., Perry, and Mamie—all married now— and retire to Polanco. Lorraine would finish out her sophomore year at Englewood, then transfer to a high school in Mexico City.

Carl stayed in Mexico while Nannie and Lorraine returned to Chicago to prepare for the move. She and Lorraine were there, together, on March 7, 1946, when they received word that Carl Hansberry had suffered a cerebral hemorrhage. He was dead at the age of fifty-one.

Lorraine, crushed and very angry, went through the next week in silent grief. Deep inside, she believed that it was racial prejudice that had killed her father—the result of fighting and winning many battles, yet losing the war.

Lorraine Hansberry said little directly about Carl's death during her lifetime. (She did address the subject in a memorable letter to the editor of the *New York Times* in 1964, in which she described her father as a "permanently embittered exile.") Yet, in another way, she wrote about nothing else. In nearly all her plays, a father's death is at the very center of the plot, moving and shaping the characters. In *A Raisin in the Sun,* Lena Younger tells her daughter-in-law Ruth, "Big Walter used to say, 'Seem like God didn't see fit to give the black man nothing but dreams—but He did give us children to make them dreams seem worthwhile.'" Big Walter, who died a few years earlier, was "a fine man, just couldn't never catch up with his dreams, that's all."

Lorraine turned sixteen shortly after Carl Hansberry's death and despite, or maybe because of, her grief, she grew quickly into a mature and defiant young woman. She continued to admire the "other" black students at school, the ones she'd stared at from the edge of the elementary school playground, those who would never be part of the Hansberrys' social circle. Racial tension was a fact of life at Englewood High—just as it was throughout Chicago—and when trouble finally came, in the form of a full-blown race riot, Lorraine was struck that she and the other "well-dressed" black students stood by as observers. They could only watch as carloads of students from all-black high schools like Wendell Phillips and

DuSable arrived to support Englewood's blacks in their war on the white students—the "ofays," as they were called. There they were, Lorraine wrote in her journal, working-class girls in tight skirts and colored anklets, held up with rubber bands—and they were ready to fight.

During those years, Lorraine immersed herself in African and African American culture. She loved reading books recommended to her by Uncle Leo, which made the "dark continent" come alive. At school, English and history classes absorbed her attention, but she let the other subjects slide without concern. Lorraine also discovered the plays of William Shakespeare under the tutelage of a "strange and bewigged teacher who we... naturally and cruelly christened 'Pale Hecate.'" ("God rest her gentle, enraptured, and igniting soul!" Lorraine added.) Pale Hecate, it seemed, did not like average work from students who could do much, much better. She accused Lorraine Hansberry of being a cheat—of cheating, that is, not only herself but the world as well. When Lorraine finally gave herself over to memorizing lines from *Macbeth* and *Julius Caesar,* she found it a "thrilling source of contact with life."

At this time, too, she began to go out with boys in her class, sometimes in groups, sometimes alone. She enjoyed these occasions, yet dating seemed so different for her than it had been for Mamie. Her sister was at the epicenter of a social whirl and her bubbly femininity seemed to attract boys by the dozens. Lorraine liked boys who shared her interests in books and politics, and who could be friends. On one of her first unchaperoned evenings, she and a date decided to integrate a previously whites-only restaurant. On an even more memorable date, a young man took her to the theater. It was her first *real* play, not a school or community production but something true and good. It was the folk musical *Dark of the Moon,* written by William Berney. Lorraine never forgot the moment when the curtain rose, the lights dimmed, and before her was the outline of the Smoky Mountains. In the dark of the moon, she watched John, the witch-boy, woo Barbara Allen. The performance was a magical mix of music and dancing and witchcraft and, by the end, Lorraine was spellbound. She adored all the "theatricality," as she called it.

From then on, she and a group of friends began to go to the theater as often as they could, riding the elevated trains into downtown Chicago to see productions of Shakespeare and works by new playwrights like Tennessee Williams and Eugene O'Neill. "The theater came into my life like—pow!" she told an interviewer. "Mine was the same old story—sort of hanging around little acting groups and developing the feeling that the theater embraces everything I like all at one time."

Less than two years later, in January 1948, Lorraine Hansberry graduated from Englewood High School. She was, as the yearbook noted, President of Forum, Gym Secretary, and eager to become a journalist. There was more, of course, to Lorraine Hansberry than those few lines beneath her senior picture. For one, despite her neat, pulled-back hair, and matching skirt and sweater, she had become a radical. And she had designs on revolution.

FIVE

Wisconsin

I was seventeen and I did not think then of *writing*
the melody as I knew it—in a different key; but I
believe it entered my consciousness and stayed
there....

—Lorraine Hansberry,
To Be Young, Gifted, and Black

IT WAS FEBRUARY 1948 and there was snow—glorious,
cold, clean Wisconsin snow. There was something
about the snow that summoned blood feelings from deep
within Lorraine. Maybe it was her European blood, she
thought, from the slave master who willed himself to be
her great-grandfather. The snow, Lorraine Hansberry
wrote later, was the only thing about life at the University
of Wisconsin that didn't disappoint her.

College life had started promisingly enough. Just after
graduating from Englewood High School in January,
Lorraine, her sister Mamie, and her brother Perry loaded
up the car and set off on the 150-mile drive north from

Chicago to Madison. The three talked and laughed as Mamie and Perry shared stories about their undergraduate years at Howard University. Only when the conversation slowed did her chest tighten again. Then she'd look out the car window at the wide, regular fields and see the snow and ice, and prickly stubs of corn. *It will be all right, it will be all right, it will be all right . . . .*

It was February, not the usual time to start one's freshman year. "February," in fact, was the reason given by the administration for why there wasn't a place for Lorraine in one of the campus dorms. She believed, though, that it was because she was black, not white like the snow or the rest of the student body. So she signed up to room at Langdon Manor, a two-story building just down the street from the Memorial Union and only a block from the shore of Lake Mendota.

The lake's frigid and penetrating winds caused the three to unpack the car very quickly. While Mamie and Perry carried boxes and suitcases, Lorraine called out friendly greetings to her floormates. She was relieved that they were such a cosmopolitan mix. There were Nordic-looking farm girls, to be sure, but also Asians, New Yorkers, even an Australian. Best of all, her roommate Edythe was black, and seemed likely to become a wonderful chum.

Meanwhile, Mamie began laying her sister's clothes, the ones she'd helped her pick out just a few weeks before, on the twin bed. Lorraine never understood why Mamie, who'd taken over the family business with Perry and Carl, wasted so much energy on clothes and such. "Just like Mama, a black Southern belle," Lorraine laughed

44

to herself as she continued listening to her sister's instructions on how a college girl should dress, all about matching skirts and sweaters and neatly pressed blouses. It's different in February, Mamie remarked casually, what with the boots, gloves, hats . . . all to be coordinated.

Lorraine listened to Mamie's parting advice, thanked her unconvincingly, then hugged her sister and brother good-bye. As soon as they were gone, she gathered up the clothes from the bed and stuffed them into her small closet. Then she lay back on the bed, lit a cigarette, and started a conversation with Edythe that lasted into the night.

Their long conversations about politics, race, art, music, literature, and life went on for much of the next two years. Housemates joined in, as well as other black students and many African exchange students. They listened to jazz and the blues, and read poetry aloud. They argued about the presidential elections of 1948, and whether to support President Harry Truman or the Progressive party's candidate, Henry Wallace. Wallace was much more sympathetic to the needs of black Americans, but he couldn't win, many said. Lorraine hated such defeatist talk. If he's good for blacks, she argued passionately, then we must support him. These discussions often ended at daybreak, after many pots of coffee and endless cigarettes.

The daytime was less certain for Lorraine. The university's core requirements forced her to study science and math as well as art and history. Her public-school deficiencies in math and science nagged at her, and she fell behind in several required courses. Something called "Physical Geography," she wrote later, particularly bedeviled her. She thought she was signing up for something that would enlighten her about the people of the world but instead was "forced" to spend hours a week hitting rocks with a little metal hammer. The point, as she wrote, simply eluded her. The worst of it was that none of her classes left her time for writing, which she was beginning to think was what she really wanted to do with her life.

She considered leaving the university altogether, after only one semester, and started imagining how she would explain this to her family. What I really want to do is study art, she practiced saying, or become a sculptor, or go to Mexico or New York, maybe become a writer? If she wasn't sure herself, she worried, how could she describe it to the rest of her family?

Then, just before her eighteenth birthday, she walked, quite by accident, as she later recalled, into the University Theater. A rehearsal for a student production of Sean O'Casey's play *Juno and the Paycock* was in progress. She approached the stage.

> Oh Blessed virgin, where were you when me darlin son was riddled with bullets—when me darlin's son was riddled with bullets.

She took a seat in the front row and moved her whole body forward. The melody of the words seemed to wash over her.

> Sacred heart of the Crucified Jesus, take away our hearts o' stone ... an' give us hearts of flesh .... Take away this murdherin' hate ... an'give us Thine own eternal love!

Juno O'Boyle's low moan hit Lorraine in a place deep

inside. "A woman's voice," she wrote later, "a howl, a shriek of misery fitted to a wail of poetry that consumed all my senses and all my awareness of human pain, endurance, and the futility of it .... How had O'Casey done it?" she wondered. How had he made Juno's despair at her son's death jump off the stage and into her own gut? How had he made this mother's tragedy ring true from generation to generation, and from culture to culture? She, a black American in 1948, felt as though she knew this Irish woman of 1916. She seemed to understand her sorrow, her strength, and her will to survive.

Lorraine longed to give this same voice to her own people. She began to think more and more about an idea for a play. Writing a play was one of many ideas that swirled about her head, but now it seemed to take shape. Hers, too, would be about tenement life, although in Chicago. In her play, there would also be kindness, poverty, irresponsibility, treachery, deceit, nobility, and love.

She jumped into the study of theater. She read the works of Swedish playwright August Strindberg and Norwegian Henrik Ibsen, both of whom had introduced social problems into their characters' worlds. Her whole being was bursting with excitement for the things she wanted to know and do. She went home for the summer, intending to return and study as much theater as she could.

In the fall, Lorraine enrolled in a set design class. She also became very active in the presidential campaign of Henry Wallace. Wallace, a former cabinet secretary under Franklin D. Roosevelt, was running against Democratic Party candidate Harry S. Truman as a member of the

Progressive party. The main platform of this third party, officially called the Progressive Citizens of America, was to end the policies of confrontation with the Soviet Union. The focus of the 1947 "Truman Doctrine," on the other hand, was that Communism must be contained at all costs. In other words, the nations of the world were either allied with the United States, or with the Soviet Union—there was no in-between. In those edgy pre-Cold War days, the Progressives were often linked with the Communists, at least by the Republican and Democratic parties.

The campaign was extraordinarily bitter. More than once Henry Wallace was pelted with eggs while giving a speech. He was taunted and jeered everywhere he went. Lorraine, who had become Wallace's university campaign chairman, felt this rejection acutely. In November, Wallace was a distant third behind Democrat Truman— who was elected President—and Republican Thomas Dewey. Lorraine's faith that anything could be achieved through the electoral process tumbled with the Wallace campaign. Her politics became more radical as she rejected anything resembling "business as usual." After all, hadn't her father spent his whole life playing by the rules, only to die exiled and embittered? She continued working for the Progressives, however, among whom she counted many friends.

She began to explore the political potential of the theater. Hadn't her own heart been more affected by Juno's wail than any candidate's speech? Unfortunately, she found that more doors were closed at the university than opened. The professor of her set design class gave her a D, even though he considered her work above average. Why encourage a black woman, he explained to her, to enter a field that was virtually all-white?

She also continued to struggle with her required classes. Her grades reflected her academic imbalance: She received "A"s in literature, history, and the fine arts, and "F"s in science and math. By the end of her freshman year, in January 1949, she'd just barely managed to pass to the sophomore level.

There were many African students among Lorraine's friends at the University of Wisconsin. She'd been fascinated with Africa and the Pan-African movement ever since her Uncle Leo's dinner-table conversations. Now, a few years after Europe's colonies in the Middle East and Asia had fought successfully for independence, Africa's time had finally come. The British, French, and Belgians, however, were reluctant to give up their last colonies. They trusted that the Kenyans, Nigerians, and Congolese, for example, lacked the commitment to fight for an African Africa. But they were wrong. Lorraine read all she could by and about new leaders like Kenya's Jomo Kenyatta and Ghana's Kwame Nkrumah (who had been one of Uncle Leo's students at Howard University). She learned the tribal songs and dances of the Kikuyu, Ashanti, Yoruba, and Mandingo, and she rejoiced in her rich cultural heritage.

As Lorraine's extracurricular life became richer and more sustaining, her required classes were unbearable. She felt the whole world was out there, waiting for her to seize hold of it, while she plugged along at a sluggish pace. She considered not returning for the spring semester of her sophomore year. She mentioned it to her family, and to her surprise they were supportive.

Yet she returned to Madison in January 1950, determined to try to finish her degree.

That month, the campus was abuzz about the opening of a new theater at the lakefront Memorial Union. The renowned architect Frank Lloyd Wright was coming to Madison to speak at the event. A Wisconsin native, Wright was both adored and reviled in Madison. Lorraine sat in the audience as Wright, an artistic icon, brilliant and a little mad, walked into the theater wearing his trademark porkpie hat, a black cape, and a string tie, surrounded by an entourage of very sophisticated and knowing young men and women. He stood at the podium and looked around the new theater. "It's rubbish," he pronounced. "It looks just like a cheesebox." And then he launched into an attack on not only the new building but the entire University of Wisconsin.

Lorraine was captivated. This famous man was so ungrateful, so inflammatory, so wickedly nasty in the honesty of his remarks. As soon as Lorraine walked through the doors of the theater, she felt a blast of cold wind off Lake Mendota. She looked out at its frozen expanse, at the snow, and she smiled. Then she ran back to Langdon Manor to tell her news. She was leaving the university forever.

SIX

Harlem

Dark Harlem waits for you.
The bus, the sub—
Pay-nights a taxi
Through the park.
O, drums of life in Harlem after dark!
O, dreams!
O, songs!
O, saxophones at night!
O, sweet relief from faces that are white!

—Langston Hughes, "Negro Servant"

When Lorraine returned to Chicago from Madison in the early months of 1950, she was still unsure of her life's course. She studied art at Roosevelt College and the Art Institute of Chicago before traveling to Mexico with her mother. By the fall, however, she'd made yet another decision. She still didn't know exactly what she would do with her life, but she did know where she wanted to live—in New York City.

Lorraine longed to be in Harlem, in the thick of the life of her people. She'd dreamed about Harlem ever since she first read Langston Hughes' poetry. Harlem was a Renaissance city, every bit as important to the new black consciousness as Florence was to the old European.

As the Twentieth Century Limited pulled out of Union Station, she felt as though she were walking right to the end of a diving board. Chicago was the edge from which she jumped hard, and then bounced right into the heart of Manhattan. New York City knows nothing about me, Lorraine thought with some exhiliration. Here I have no past, only a future. Together with three other young women, Lorraine moved into an apartment on Manhattan's Lower East Side ("to my total dissatisfaction," she wrote to Edythe in Madison. "Would prefer to live in Harlem, however, but it is too damn crowded in the ghetto for even those who want to move in. . ."). She enrolled in classes at the New School for Social Research and began writing articles for the *Young Progressives of America* magazine. Within days of arriving in the city she made her way to Harlem, and was immediately caught in its magical web. She walked its streets as a happy outsider, taking in its brashness, gaiety, and raucousness. She felt like a tuning fork, her senses reverberating at the slightest sensation.

For any aspiring artist, New York City was a heady place to be in 1950. Just as most Americans were enjoying the unprecedented prosperity following World War II and viewing their lives with considerable smugness, New York's artistic community was challenging the authenticity of the "good life." In 1949, Arthur Miller's play *Death of a Salesman* caused a furor when it charged that America's middle-class values were hollow. Two years earlier, in 1947, Tennessee Williams had exposed the tears in Southern society with the searing *A Streetcar Named Desire.* Since Williams' first success, in 1945, with *The Glass Menagerie,* his plays both attracted and repulsed audiences with their strains of violence and undertones of social criticism.

Among black artists, Ralph Ellison and Langston Hughes were at the center of attention. Lorraine had read Mr. Hughes' poems over and over since the days when he came to call at her family's home on South Park Way. She had always loved the way he turned everyday black experience into poetry: "When Sue Wears Red," "Song to a Negro Washwoman," "Mother to Son," and "Heart of Harlem." In Harlem, his poems seemed more vital and vibrant than ever. He *was* Harlem, famous for walking up and down the streets, making friends wherever he went. Everyone, it seemed, knew Mr. Hughes.

In 1950 Harlem, or any urban black community, was truly a world apart from the rest of America. During the early Cold War years, many Americans viewed the world in facile absolutes: Right versus Wrong, Capitalism versus Communism, the United States versus the Soviet Union. What black activists and artists knew all too well, however, was that they were assumed to be on the "wrong" side of those issues. In the U.S. Senate, Joseph McCarthy began his search for "un-American" activities, and plunged the country into an anticommunist fervor. Helped considerably by FBI Director J. Edgar Hoover, McCarthy cast a wide internal security net over American society, hoping to catch many of those whose politics couldn't be neatly explained and categorized.

During the early 1950s, the mere fact of being black made one a subversive, not quite an "American." The South's Jim Crow laws were attacked vigorously in Harlem, for example, while in the rest of the United States they weren't seriously questioned. Black activists were viewed as uppity, and both the police and the FBI were alert to suspicious activity—which included any criticism of U.S. policy on almost any issue. "I know many who have already been lapped up by this new Reich terror," Lorraine wrote to her former roommate Edythe. "Know the arrests in the early morning, the shiftyeyed ones who follow, follow, follow (and know the people who are the victims: the quiet and the courageous. . . ."

Early in 1951, Lorraine was offered a job on the newspaper *Freedom,* founded just a few months earlier by a Hansberry family friend, Paul Robeson. Prevented by government harassment from lecturing and performing around the country, Robeson turned to journalism as a way to get his message out. "Where One Is Enslaved, All Are in Chains," read the paper's masthead. *"Freedom,"* Lorraine wrote Edythe, "ought to be the journal of Negro liberation . . . in fact, it will be." Its editorial goal was similar to that of Robert Abbott's Chicago *Defender,* founded fifty years earlier: to keep the black community informed of news that directly affected them, which the white mainstream press would never cover.

Lorraine began by doing a bit of everything—typing, office work, writing. She submitted her assigned stories to the editor, Louis Burnham, an "altogether commanding personality,"who had formerly been the Southern director of the Progressive Party. Mr. Burnham sat behind a desk in front of a large curved window, from which one could see much of Harlem. There was little in the room, Lorraine remembered, except Mr. Burnham and that view, but they complemented one another perfectly.

Lorraine was only twenty at the time of her first meeting with Louis Burnham. She immediately launched into a description of the novel she'd begun writing two years earlier. Now that she'd seen so much more of life, the ugly side, she told him, she wondered if she was still innocent enough to continue her book. "It was part of his genius as a human being that he did not laugh at all, or patronize my dilemma," she later wrote. He became her mentor, teaching her about both journalism and the very nature of racism—"rotten, white or black"—and that *everything* is political.

Recognizing the precociousness of Lorraine's talent, Louis Burnham gave her assignments that encouraged both her journalistic and political growth. He sent her all over Harlem, whose sights, sounds, and smells she found as vital to life as her own breath. She felt her family's heritage of activism grow strong within her, although hers was a more feisty version.

One bright summer afternoon Lorraine was sent to a local Baptist church to cover a funeral. She arrived early and sat near the back, ready with pad of paper and pencil to record her thoughts. It wasn't Sunday, she noted, but it might as well have been. Many people, dressed in suits and dresses and large hats, had crowded into the overheated church. They fanned themselves, looking around uncomfortably. Something was wrong. Finally, someone rushed in, and, in a low voice, asked if anyone would please go to the undertaker's and see what was taking so long. Lorraine stood up and went toward the man. She was quickly driven through the Harlem streets to a dank funeral home. Inside all was dark and quiet. A voice asked, "Why have you come?" "Everyone's waiting," she replied. The undertaker said he was almost ready. Lorraine walked over to the open casket and looked in. He was just a teenager, part of a student protest. "How had it happened?" someone asked. "Cops," Lorraine answered unhesitatingly. It was, as she later noted, "official violence."

"People say to me, what makes you so suspicious?" she wrote to Edythe. "Ha! In this world to think some even dare ask!" Paul Robeson, Langston Hughes, and W. E. B. DuBois, men she'd known and known about all her life, as real to her as her own dear father, were hounded and dishonored. Lesser-known figures simply disappeared, forced underground. Their lifelong struggle for justice and freedom was actively discredited by the government, which ignorantly lumped them all together as "Communist sympathizers." Anyone, it seemed, with leftist connections or who dared criticize the government in any way was considered a security threat. By 1954, J. Edgar Hoover's FBI had 26,000 names on their security index, people who were suspected of being "unAmerican." Robeson, Hughes, and DuBois were all on that list. So was Lorraine Hansberry.

Yet, despite such obvious injustices, activists seemed powerless against the forces of McCarthyism. Hundreds were called before the Wisconsin senator's infamous

House Un-American Activities Committee (HUAC) and asked, "Are you, or have you ever been, a member of the Communist Party?" It didn't matter if they answered "No," which they nearly always did. Being called before the committee was a sign of implicit guilt, and many immediately lost their jobs—teaching positions withdrawn, speaking engagements and book contracts canceled—and sometimes they lost their homes and families as well.

Paul Robeson was under continued attack and eventually his passport was revoked by the State Department for his suspected Communist leanings. In March 1952, Lorraine took Robeson's place at an international peace conference in Montevideo, Uruguay, and delivered the speech he was to give. After a very scary plane ride, which saw the start of her lifelong fear of flying, she was given bouquets of flowers, small gifts, and cheered as though she were as famous as "Señor Robeson." After she delivered his speech, the audience jumped to its feet in appreciation. It was, to say the least, a heady experience for a twenty-two-year-old.

Back in New York, Lorraine threw herself into her *Freedom* stories with a zeal that never questioned that this was the most important work in the world. She covered boycotts, meetings, and demonstrations, and attended rallies at places like the Rockland Palace and the Golden Gate Ballroom. She gave impromptu speeches at the corner of 125th Street and Seventh Avenue in front of Michaux's Book Store, which boasted of containing, "A Hundred Thousand Facts about the Negro."

In December 1952, Lorraine was named *Freedom*'s associate editor. Her work at the paper, she liked to say, was her *real* college education. She became essayist, theater critic, book reviewer, and social analyst, covering political repression throughout the world. The paper put itself in the forefront of the discussion of the new African nations and their efforts to win freedom from Europe's colonial powers. They published, for example, a detailed map of Africa that showed English, French, and American interests in tin, iron ore, and diamonds, and the great variety of native peoples and languages. Of the twenty-five articles she contributed to the paper, one of her favorites was "Kenya's Kikuyus," in which she mixed African folktale and political reality.

Lorraine had been an astute observer of Africa since high school, when her Uncle Leo spoke so engagingly about the continent's people. Louis Burnham recognized her keen understanding and assigned her to cover such important topics of the day as the struggle for independence in the Gold Coast, later returned to its African name, Ghana, and its dynamic leader, Kwame Nkrumah. Dr. Nkrumah, who had studied African history with Lorraine's Uncle Leo at Howard University, was imprisoned by the British in 1951 for leading a general strike. Yet, while in prison, he was elected Prime Minister. "The promise of the future of Ghana," she wrote, "is the promise of freedom."

Harlem's flamboyant Congressman Adam Clayton Powell, City Councilman Benjamin Davis, and, of course, Paul Robeson, were all there to teach Lorraine about struggle and commitment. They encouraged her to cover education, juvenile crime, and labor disputes. She learned to write fast and to go beneath the surface, where the subjects of her interviews often didn't want her to go.

These years also brought definition to Lorraine's two selves. One was the anxious interior self, the youngest child with much to prove and nagging self-doubt. The exterior Lorraine, however, was committed, energetic, and very outspoken. It was this insolent Lorraine who walked the Harlem streets reporting on crime and school quality, following the pulse of the neighborhood. She scribbled notes all day, then wrote and revised late into the night. "I'm considerably slimmer than you remember me," she wrote in a letter to Edythe. "And I think I smile less, but perhaps with more sincerity when I do."

Still, despite Lorraine's maturity and independence, when her mother and sister visited New York during her second year there, they were frankly worried. What kind of life is this, Nannie Hansberry wondered, for a nice middle-class girl? She pressed Lorraine on the subject of marriage, which Lorraine promptly scorned. Lorraine was exasperated with her mother and sister. Did they really think there was nothing else to life besides a house and a husband?

Still, a few months later, while protesting the exclusion of blacks from the New York University basketball team, Lorraine met a young NYU graduate student in English named Robert Nemiroff. He was, she told a friend the very next day, "a very nice person." He was also an aspiring writer and fellow lover of books, politics, and the world of ideas. He liked to talk but he knew how to listen, too. They began taking long walks together, talking on and on about their passions, often stopping at small ethnic restaurants where the conversation, and outrageous laughter, continued. Bob seemed immediately to recognize and understand Lorraine's two sides: the clown and the intellectual. With him, she felt completely comfortable being both, as she wrote, "a chattering, guitar-playing, slow-drag dancing, guzzling figure of renaissance well-being" and the "serious odd-talking kid."

On the outside, there seemed more differences between the two than similarities. Bob was white, and his parents were first-generation Russian Jews who managed several New York restaurants. Yet both Lorraine and Bob were committed artists and activists who quickly discovered that being together, whether it was to go to plays or poetry readings, or to protest unfair housing practices or police brutality, was much nicer than being apart. Bob had two sides, too. One was absent-minded, even bumbling. He was a laughingly bad dresser; as one friend remembered, he "never seemed to get it right; wrong tie with right jacket; short black socks exposing white flesh; wrinkled everything. . . ." Yet about art and, increasingly, Lorraine's art, he was intense and focused. Even as a young man, he was able to sort out the important things in life and always keep them ahead of the trivial.

Gradually, Bob's name was mentioned more and more in Lorraine's letters to her family in Chicago. After a while, Lorraine was pleased to be able to say that, yes, Mama, there *is* someone I'd like to settle down with. To Edythe she sent a brief note. "Supposed to get married about September. Spirit: Happy and defiant."

SEVEN

A Terrific, No, Exciting,
Idea for a Plazy . . .

My work. It is only here on paper that I dare say it
like that. "My work!". . . Oh, what I think I must
tell this world! Oh the time that I crave—and the
peace—and the *power.*

—Lorraine Hansberry,
journal entry, Christmas 1955

ROBERT NEMIROFF was probably not what Nannie
Hansberry had in mind when she pleaded with
Lorraine to be a good middle-class girl and find herself a
husband. Still, given what Mrs. Hansberry knew of her
youngest child's resistance to anything "normal," she
didn't quibble about his being either white or Jewish or a
decided New Yorker. She kept her peace, knowing that
one word of criticism might have caused her daughter to
remain single forever. When Nannie and Mamie visited
Lorraine in New York early in 1953, they "could see," as

Mamie remembered, "that he was just an adorable person, and he was completely open and free."

Bobby, as Lorraine called him, was just a few months older than her. His parents, Russian Jewish immigrants who spoke heavily accented English, had suffered terribly during the Depression. By the 1950s, however, they owned several successful restaurants and were prosperous New Yorkers. They warmly accepted Lorraine into their family.

Still, despite Lorraine's love for Bobby, she had misgivings about marriage. "Should I marry *anyone?*" she often wondered. She wanted to be completely sure she wasn't taking this step just to please her mother or even society at large, which, during the 1950s, believed women should marry. Period.

During Christmas 1952, Lorraine returned to Chicago alone. On December 26, she wrote Bobby that the long train trip had allowed her to clear her head and focus on matters both romantic and artistic: "I have finally admitted to myself," she wrote, "that I do love you and that I have a terrific, *no, exciting,* idea for a play."

Less than a year after their first meeting, Lorraine and Bobby were happily planning their lives together. They agreed to devote themselves to art, theater, music, and, of course, remaking the world. Both the Hansberry and Nemiroff families seemed remarkably relaxed about the union, especially, as Mamie said, considering their family hadn't "done anything interracial really with someone immediately in our family." Nannie's misgivings, in fact, were considerable, especially given that at the time interracial marriage was illegal in thirty states. Nannie, who naturally assumed Lorraine and Bob would have children one day, was wise enough to know that the world can be unkind to those who don't belong to one group or another. Still, everyone loved Bobby and could see that he made Lorraine very happy. And Bob's own parents, Mae and Motya, and his brother and sister had accepted Lorraine completely. In the end, the Hansberrys and the Nemiroffs chose to look beyond their obvious differences and embrace the many similarities.

Lorraine and Bob decided to have their wedding in Chicago, although they insisted it be a very low-key affair. Of course, it wasn't. Nannie did have it in the family home, as Lorraine requested, but her idea of informality was decidedly different from Lorraine's. The guest list was long, and when Lorraine and Bob arrived, tired after a long drive from New York, the house was filled with flowers, presents, and the buzz of an imminent production.

The day before their wedding, June 19, 1953, the bride and groom spent the day picketing outside the Chicago Federal Building. They were protesting the imminent execution of Ethel and Julius Rosenberg, who had been found guilty of passing top-secret information on nuclear weapons to the Soviet Union. The Rosenberg case had become an international cause célèbre, and many believed the couple's harsh sentence was a result of Cold War hysteria. Throughout the country, protesters maintained deathwatch vigils, holding out hope that President Dwight D. Eisenhower would grant executive clemency. He didn't, and the Rosenbergs were put to death during the night.

Robert Nemiroff later recalled that emotional exhaustion from the long protest nearly caused them to postpone the ceremony. Since, however, both families had clearly gone to considerable expense and trouble, they decided to proceed. At 6:30 in the evening on June 20, Lorraine entered her mother's living room, unescorted, wearing the white lacy dress Mamie had picked out for her own wedding several years earlier. Lorraine, looking tired but very happy, crossed the room to the white brick fireplace, where Bob stood next to Reverend Archibald M. Carey, a Chicago city councilman who later became a United States delegate to the United Nations. Following the brief ceremony, the guests sat down to a lavish dinner. Then, the next day, the newlyweds drove back to their busy lives in New York City.

About a month later, they moved into a small apartment on Bleecker Street in New York's Greenwich Village. The "Village," whose crooked, narrow streets and low buildings contrasted with the wide avenues and skyscrapers of the rest of Manhattan, had long been a refuge for artists. Lorraine and Bob loved their cramped, book- and record-filled apartment just above a small store with a huge sign, "Joe's Hand Laundry."

During the first year of their marriage, they each held several jobs. Lorraine worked as a typist, receptionist, and assistant at the folk music magazine *Sing Out,* which first published Woody Guthrie's "This Land Is Your Land" and the black anthem "We Shall Overcome." She also continued to contribute frequent articles to *Freedom* until the newspaper stopped publication in 1955. Bob completed his master's degree at NYU and then became a reader for the Sears Reading Club. He later worked as an editor and promotion director for Avon Books.

Both agreed that jobs were only for generating money to cover living expenses. Their life's work was elsewhere, either in the projects piled on desks or tabletops throughout their apartment or in the creative whirl that was Greenwich Village during the 1950s. Robert and Lorraine took in as much of it as they could—folk concerts in Washington Square, poetry readings in coffeehouses, plays, movies, and art exhibits. On their few quiet evenings at home, Lorraine began to sketch out her ideas for her first play. It was one she'd been thinking about for a long time. Perhaps now, she thought, is the time to start writing.

In 1955, Robert Nemiroff and a close friend, Burt D'Lugoff, collaborated on a funny little song they called "Cindy, Oh, Cindy." Mamie Hansberry Mitchell recalled how when Bob and Lorraine returned to Chicago that Christmas, Bob pulled out his guitar and taught everyone his song. They all sat around singing about Cindy and "sniggering and giggling," as Mamie remembered.

They stopped laughing, however, when in August 1956, "Cindy" was released and made its way onto the radio. Within a few months Robert Nemiroff had made $100,000 from his silly little song, and Lorraine was set free from her string of odd jobs. She could now devote herself full-time to writing her play. As Bob wrote on the inside of a drama anthology he gave her for her twenty-sixth birthday, "From Shakespeare to Shaw . . . because one day, if you work hard enough at it (and cut out the nonsense) you may be up there among them. . . ."

Bob's support had always been crucial to Lorraine's writing, even before she was bold enough to call it "my work." He understood the needs of a writer—emotional support, privacy, time—and gave Lorraine all he could. He seemed to understand, and love, her complexities and contradictions. With Bobby, Lorraine shared the burden of all her fears, and they were many. She was afraid of heights, water, boats, bridges, tunnels, and airplanes. "I can tell you now that was a positively horrible Saturday that you all left on that damn thing," she wrote Bobby while he was on a business trip. "It seemed to me every plane near that airport almost smashed into something before I got away from the area. . . . YOU ARE NEVER TO FLY AGAIN."

At first, Lorraine worked on several plays at once, before finally focusing her energies on the one that became *A Raisin in the Sun.* After she finished the first draft, she let Bob read it. Encouraged by his evaluation, she plunged ahead, convinced that this was "the one." During an eight-month period between her twenty-sixth and twenty-seventh birthdays, she worked on it nearly around the clock. She slept and ate little, smoked countless cigarettes, and drank pots of strong coffee. It was a long process of giving birth, and the labor was very difficult.

The gestation period, too, had been long, perhaps more than twenty years. She'd been imagining the Younger family—Mama, Walter Lee, Ruth, and Beneatha—since she'd stood at the edge of her elementary school playground and looked on admiringly as her classmates swaggered and talked tough. She couldn't be like them, she knew, but she understood their pain, and could try to give them a voice.

The setting would be Chicago, of that she was certain. She knew it well; it was her city, the way Dublin was Sean O'Casey's. Chicago was brutal and raw and it presented challenges to the characters every bit as demanding as their relationships with each other. Within the city, there would be an apartment, a "kitchenette." Lorraine knew all about these, too, of course. Thirty years after her own father had created kitchenettes as an answer to the Depression's acute housing shortage, they had become rat traps. Any family still living in one, Lorraine knew, would be troubled spiritually, if not in a thousand other ways as well. As she writes in her stage directions about the Youngers' apartment, "Weariness has, in fact, won in this room."

Her characters would be members of one family, the Youngers, but they would be different from the Hansberrys. The Youngers worked hard for little reward; there would be no white fur coats under the Christmas tree for them. One explanation for the decision to tell a working-class story appears in a book review she wrote for *Freedom*. In her piece, she criticized Howard Fast's best-selling book *Spartacus* because his story of Roman slaves was not told from the slave's point of view. The slaves, she noted, are the real heroes of these historical tales, since those who have nothing must always live heroically.

Lorraine was less sure about other details, although she did have a title. It was going to be called *The Crystal Stair*, after the poem "Mother to Son" by Langston Hughes:

Well, son, I'll tell you:
Life for me ain't been no crystal stair.
It's had tacks in it,
and splinters,
and boards torn up,
and places with no carpet on the floor
Bare.

Mama could have said those words to her son, Walter Lee, Lorraine thought, as she watched him be crushed by life's disappointments. Still, the play's creation did not follow a straight line from start to finish. If it followed a line at all, it was one that darted up and down. And then sometimes, at the bottom, the line, smudged by distraction, threatened never to rise again. "All told, I have been fairly bored and lonely," she wrote to Bob when he left her alone for a few days. "Wish to God I could drink. (I have reread my play a couple of times to my disgust. Had a new idea—a libretto. But have quietly resolved—yes, I will piddle around with a libretto after (1) the play is finished . . .)."

As her long nights of writing passed, one after the other, Lorraine grappled with several issues: Who is the main character—Walter Lee or Mama? Or is there no main character at all? Should she model specific characters after her own family, or even after herself? (Could she help it?) And, just what were the points she wanted to make? She huddled over her characters like a sculptor, carefully chiseling every feature. Finally, she was able to write to Bob: "Much of it *is* labored—much, however, reads well—and for the first time, begins to approximate what I thought I wanted to say. Above all, I am beginning to think of the people as *people*. . . ."

Lena Younger—Mama—carries the weight of five generations of slaves and sharecroppers. She's a survivor and, like Lorraine's own mother, the product of another, more deferential time. When Mama—and Nannie Perry—grew up, there were more certainties and they both had learned them well. Yet Lena Younger can't seem to pass her wisdom on to her children, Walter Lee and Beneatha, who insist on doing everything their own way.

All Walter Lee seems to want is money, like the white man. ("Once upon a time freedom used to be life—now it's money. I guess the world really do change," Mama laments.) Walter carries the huge weight of his own disappointments, and that's enough to crush him. He thinks money will save him, and when the family gets $10,000 from his dead father's life insurance policy, Walter Lee's sure he can set himself up for life. When he's swindled out of the money, he announces proudly that he's learned the only lesson worth learning: There's no God, there's just the "man." "It's all divided up. Life is," he explains, "between the takers and the 'tooken.'"

Walter Lee has also figured out one other problem—women. Specifically, the women in his family, including his wife Ruth. They demand and complain and don't understand about "building their men up and making 'em feel like they somebody."

Beneatha, whom Lorraine later tells an interviewer is "me eight years ago," is flighty, inconsistent, and very passionate, especially about medicine and Africa. She has formed a close friendship with a Nigerian student named

Asagai, who is articulate and regal and, in Beneatha's eyes, towers over Walter Lee in every way.

Night after sleepless night, Lorraine shepherded Mama, Walter Lee, Beneatha, and Ruth through her well-ordered play. She wanted to lift them off the manuscript pages and force readers and audiences to care. She was going to be criticized, she knew, for the play's tidy structure, which was not at all avant-garde, like so many other plays of the day. People would call her a hopeless idealist, she knew, for not viewing the world as both complicated and overwhelming and her characters as victims. Like Sean O'Casey, though, Lorraine didn't want to portray life's confusion but humanity's power and nobility.

She had been seventeen when she first heard Juno Boyle cry out over the loss of her son in Sean O'Casey's play *Juno and the Paycock:* "Sacred Heart of the Crucified Jesus, take away our hearts o'stone...an' give us hearts of flesh!" That wail had entered deep into her consciousness. "I did not think then of writing the melody as I knew it—in a different key...." Ten years later, however, she had her melody: "When you starts measuring somebody," Mama says in the play's last act, "measure him right, child, measure him right. Make sure you done taken into account what hills and valleys he come through before he got to wherever he is."

Gradually Lorraine began to realize that *The Crystal Stair* was a play about dreams—having them and keeping them, even in the face of crushing frustration. She wanted a new title, one that suggested this theme, and so she turned back to Langston Hughes. She found just what she was looking for:

What happens to a dream deferred?
Does it dry up
like a raisin in the sun?
Or fester like a sore—And then run?
Does it stink like rotten meat?
Or crust and sugar over
like a syrupy sweet?
Maybe it just sags
like a heavy load.
Or does it explode?

She would call her play *A Raisin in the Sun*, after the withered dreams of her characters, of her people, and even, maybe especially, of her father. Lorraine dedicated the play to her own Mama, who had armed herself against the threatening white mobs nearly twenty years before. Yet Carl Hansberry's legacy of hard work, struggle, and dashed dreams is woven into every single page.

EIGHT

The Human Race Concerns Me . . .

HOST: Are there any particular themes that concern
you as a dramatist? Or is it more general?

L.H.: The human race concerns me and everything
that implies. . . .

—Lorraine Hansberry,
To Be Young, Gifted, and Black

DURING THE TIME that Lorraine was writing her play,
America was in the happy grip of a new form of entertainment—television. Many Americans spent hours
every week watching the small black-and-white screen
that sat inside a big paneled box. They laughed at the
bright clown *Howdy Doody* and at *I Love Lucy,* cried at dramas on *Hallmark Hall of Fame,* and grew increasingly
angry at news footage from places like Alabama, Mississippi, and Arkansas. The civil rights movement was the
first major ongoing story to be covered by television.

In December 1955, Rosa Parks, a department store
seamstress in Montgomery, Alabama, boarded a bus at the

end of a long workday and took a seat in the back. A few stops later, the bus was full. Since by law any black person was obligated to give their seat to any white person, Rosa was asked by the bus driver to leave her seat. She refused. She was tired, she explained, she'd paid her fare, and she intended to stay seated until she got to her stop. Rosa, whose unassuming manner masked a steely determination, was arrested and taken to jail. Within a few days, a group of civil rights activists, including a young Baptist minister named Martin Luther King, Jr., organized a boycott of the Montgomery bus system. This thirteen-month-long boycott was characterized by crude and violent behavior by Montgomery's white citizens. America watched it all on television with growing fascination.

In the fall of 1957, nine black students attempted to begin classes at Little Rock's all-white Central High School. The landmark Supreme Court decision *Brown v. Topeka* or (*Brown v. Board of Education,* as it is more commonly known), made school segregation illegal; yet, in the South, integration of local schools was achieved only by force and on a school-by-school basis. When the nine students attempted to enter Central High, the Governor of Arkansas called out the Arkansas National Guard to block their entrance. President Eisenhower could not allow a state to block enforcement of a Supreme Court ruling, so he sent in 1,000 Army troops to escort the students to school. As the students walked past white demonstrators, they were pelted with eggs, taunted, and jeered. The rest of America watched on television.

When these scenes of violence and hatred came into the living rooms of ordinary people, the viewers were changed forever. White Americans had heard about the treatment of blacks by Southerners, but now that they were confronted with it on television, they felt outrage, sympathy, and guilt. Many were roused from complacency and began to wish for an end to the unjust and unnecessary suffering.

As Arkansas Governor Orval Faubus announced on nationwide television that he would do nothing to protect the black students at Central High School, Lorraine completed the first draft of *A Raisin in the Sun*. One evening a short while later, she and Robert invited an old friend, Burt D'Lugoff, Robert's "Cindy, Oh, Cindy" collaborator, and Philip Rose, a music publisher, to dinner at their apartment. Lorraine made spaghetti and served banana cream pie, and then, when the table was cleared and Spice, their "sort of collie," was locked in the bedroom to prevent interruption, she began to read her play. Lorraine remembered feeling that during that evening she gave birth to the play; it left her body and took on a life of its own. When she was done, the four talked long into the night. By the time D'Lugoff and Rose left the apartment, at nearly daybreak, they were planning how to take *A Raisin in the Sun* to Broadway.

To say the least, mounting a full-scale Broadway production for a black drama written by an unknown black woman was a remote possibility. Broadway audiences were nearly 100 percent white and any roles for blacks had been strictly for their value as "exotic entertainment," as defined by whites. (One notable exception had been the work of Paul Robeson, who appeared on Broadway in Shakespeare's *Othello* and Eugene O'Neill's *All God's*

Chillun Got Wings and *The Emperor Jones*.) The idea that blacks might have problems with which whites could empathize was so new as to seem radical. That black people themselves might come to the theater to see such a play was unimaginable. As James Baldwin said, "Black people ignored the theater because the theater had always ignored them."

All of this made *A Raisin in the Sun* seem extremely risky to potential investors. Philip Rose, however, was so smitten with the play that within days of Lorraine's reading he contacted his friend, the stage and film actor Sidney Poitier, about the role of Walter Lee Younger. Poitier, who had recently starred in the films *Cry, the Beloved Country, The Blackboard Jungle,* and *The Defiant Ones,* was moved by the part. Calling Lorraine's "fix on the black experience truly uncanny," he agreed at once. He told Philip Rose that he knew of a possible director, a talented young black man named Lloyd Richards. Before long, Ruby Dee, who had played opposite Sidney Poitier in the film *The Edge of Night* and who was a friend of Lorraine's and Bob's, was cast as Ruth Younger, and the veteran actress Claudia McNeil took the role of Mama.

Despite assembling an impressive cast, the producers had to go to extraordinary lengths to secure financing. After being turned down by every established backer in the theater business, Robert Nemiroff, Burt D'Lugoff, and another newcomer, David Cogan, used a network of friends and acquaintances, all of whom helped usher *A Raisin in the Sun* through a maze of union laws and rehearsal restrictions. Large investors were not to be found; instead, they asked a total of 147 individuals, including such well-known black artists as Harry Belafonte, to contribute $250 each. Even with the money in hand, no Broadway theater would consider even renting space to the production.

Still, there was considerable excitement, both within the production and gradually among the New York theater community as well, about the sparkling script and the talented cast and crew. Rehearsals began in New York on December 27, 1958, and a month later, the company was ready for tryouts in New Haven. Despite the sense of, as one reporter noted, "an emerging bombshell," all was not harmonious behind the scenes. Just as Lorraine had wavered on paper about whether Mama or Walter Lee should be the play's main character, so Sidney Poitier and Claudia McNeil had their own ideas on the matter. Sidney wanted Walter Lee to dominate; not surprisingly, Claudia McNeil's Mama jockeyed for the same position. Lloyd Richards, Phil Rose, and Lorraine were happy with Mama's dominance on the stage and, judging from the first reactions in New Haven, audiences agreed. Sidney Poitier's objections, however, were ironclad. He believed that if the play unfolded from Mama's point of view, Walter Lee would be weakened to the point that his character would reflect badly on all black males. He felt this so strongly, he wrote later, that he reworked his entire performance so he could play against, rather than cower before, Claudia McNeil's powerful Mama.

Lorraine tried to see Sidney's point but insisted she had not purposely written a weak male role. The glowing reviews in New Haven and then in Philadelphia hardened Lorraine, Phil, and Lloyd's resolve to "lock the play in," to call its form final. Sidney protested, and Lorraine ultimately accused him of behaving like an impetuous star who didn't want to share the audience's attention with another actor. Sidney, for his part, accused Lorraine and the producers of "smelling gold" and being reluctant to make reasonable artistic changes. The arguments lasted for hours, Sidney remembered, and eventually, he and Lorraine stopped speaking altogether.

As Robert Nemiroff wrote many years later, "The pressures were enormous (if unspoken and rarely even acknowledged in the excitement of the work) not to press fate unduly with unnecessary risks." The sacrifices— whole scenes were cut—were made simply to keep the play at a length that would be acceptable to investors and theatergoers alike. When audiences reacted warmly to Mama's character, Lorraine and the others were inclined to leave her alone.

Despite the glowing reviews in New Haven and Philadelphia, a Broadway theater was not immediately available, so the Schubert organization, which now wished to book *A Raisin in the Sun* in its Ethel Barrymore Theatre, suggested a run in Chicago. Philip Rose and David Cogan accepted the offer, and Lorraine prepared to go back to her—and to *Raisin*'s—home, this time as an "almost celebrity."

By the time the play arrived in Chicago, *A Raisin in the Sun*'s success seemed all but assured. Sidney Poitier's grumbling faded a bit, and Claudia McNeil, whose contract lasted as long as the play's New York run, allowed herself to think that the play might run for months and months. Lorraine couldn't think that far ahead. She could only think "Chicago," where the audience would be full of friends and family.

Lorraine's sister, Mamie, remembered that when people spoke of the play—and during those days who could talk of anything else?—their mother would just nod her head and beam. Yet privately her daughter's stunning success seemed to bring tears as often as smiles, tears of joy and of sadness, too. How Carl would have enjoyed this moment, she couldn't help but think, and how it would have eased some of the pain of those long-ago years when the family moved to Washington Park. At that time neither Carl nor Nannie could have known how that experience would affect their children's lives, much less that their youngest would one day pour her fear and emotional anguish into a work of art.

On opening night, Lorraine, dressed, styled, and made up to Mamie's total satisfaction, thought about Carl too. She felt his presence everywhere in the theater, not just in the plot and words of the play, but also in the knowing smiles and warm hugs of their friends. When, in the final scene, Walter Lee says with conviction: "And we have decided to move into our house because my father—my father—he earned it for us brick by brick...," Lorraine could hear gasps and sobs around her as these people— *her* people—recognized themselves in Walter's words. "We don't want to make no trouble for nobody or fight no causes and we will try to be good neighbors. And that's *all* we got to say about that...."

Lorraine, sitting with Nannie and Mamie, squeezed her mother's hand as the curtain fell. She didn't let go until the audience jumped to its feet and Lorraine, pulled from her seat, acknowledged their approval with a wave. Then the faces closed in around her and seemed to become part of a dizzying blur. She struggled to focus her eyes and make out familiar features. Where are you, Langston? she wondered. I heard you were coming tonight, how I would love to see your face! And, what about the others from the early days—Pale Hecate, Mamie's football player, the kids on the school playground who poured ink on her white fur coat? Suddenly, the house lights came up and the faces near by, in full color now, began to speak: *We just loved it . . . . Thank you, dear, thank you . . . . You captured our experience, our lives, and now the whole world will want to see . . . .*

"The Tuesday night it opened in Chicago," remembered Chicago journalist Lerone Bennett, "that was one of the most delightful evenings I've ever spent in the theater. The play . . . the *people* . . . All that richness, all that great talent on one stage . . . the totality packed a wallop."

Later that night, Mr. Bennett attended a reception at the Hansberry home. "It was that kind of party, you know, . . . an emerging celebrity, Chicago girl, and old Chicago people who hadn't seen her in a long time. . . . She was being transformed from an anonymous person into a celebrity." It wasn't a time for serious talk, as Lorraine whirled from one cluster of friends to another. They all wanted to share this moment with her, and she in turn wanted to thank them for coming, and for their support. In the end, though, after the well-wishers left, Lorraine flopped down on the couch and talked with the few remaining guests about "art and struggle" and all that she wanted to do in the future. Except, of course, at that moment, Lorraine Hansberry's future was absolutely unpredictable.

As Lorraine headed back to New York and the Broadway opening of *A Raisin in the Sun,* she couldn't help but wonder what all this—this becoming famous—would mean for her life. Of course she wanted fame, but, for example, when was the last time she'd been alone with her husband? As a producer and partner, he'd been along for this wild ride, too; yet what were his thoughts? Clearly, *Raisin* had control of both their lives and would keep it for much longer. Lorraine couldn't help but feel a twinge of anxiety. Would life together with Bob ever be the same? Could she try to hold on to what she didn't want to change?

On March 11, when the play finally opened at the Ethel Barrymore Theatre, Lorraine sat in the audience again, with her mother, sister, brothers, and their families. She wore the stunning black dress Mamie had insisted she buy in Chicago. Scattered throughout the theater were fellow artists, writers, activists, and—most importantly for Lorraine—ordinary people, black and white, who had come to see her little play. They came, as James Baldwin wrote, "because the life on that stage said something to them concerning their own lives."

As the curtain came down on the third act, the audience members rose to their feet so spontaneously and boisterously that many in the cast were moved to tears. Director Lloyd Richards walked onto the stage and then the clapping became a steady beat, and shouts of "Author, author, author," were heard throughout the theater. Ruby Dee leaned over and asked Sidney Poitier to lead Lorraine up to the stage from the audience. He jumped down and brought her from her mother's side. Standing among the cast, looking small and slightly dazed, she wasn't sure herself whether to laugh or cry.

Early that morning, the tired, giddy cast and crew gathered to read the reviews:

"It is honest drama," wrote Frank Aston in the *New York World Telegram.* "Catching up real people. It may rip you to shreds. It will make you proud of human beings."
"There is nothing more moving in *A Raisin in the Sun,*" wrote Walter Kerr in the *New York Herald Tribune,* "than the spectacle of Sidney Poitier biting his lip, clutching the back of a chair, and turning himself into a man."
"The play is honest," added Brooks Atkinson of the *New York Times.* "It is Miss Hansberry's personal contribution to an explosive situation in which simple honesty is the most difficult thing in the world. And also the most illuminating."

The timing for *Raisin*'s appearance on the national scene couldn't have been better. The civil rights movement, with Martin Luther King, Jr. as its leader, had grabbed headlines around the world. Young black students, emboldened by the actions of Rosa Parks and the Little Rock Nine, had begun to organize and stage protests and sit-ins throughout the South. They were proudly following in the footsteps of Frederick Douglass, W. E. B. DuBois, and Paul Robeson. They, like Walter Lee Younger, wanted only to be treated with ordinary human dignity.

The sit-ins and protests drew the usual response from Southern politicians and police. Students were arrested, expelled from school. One young man was kidnapped, whipped, and had the Ku Klux Klan symbol carved on his abdomen. Others were attacked by police dogs and struck by clubs and chains. Broadcast on television day after day, the images gripped the American public. It seemed too much sometimes, enough to make some whites wonder: Were they capable of such things themselves?

At the same time, both whites and blacks flocked to see *A Raisin in the Sun,* both at its out-of-town tryouts and on Broadway. Blue-collar workers from Harlem, Brooklyn, and the Bronx joined society matrons from Westchester County. How they loved Mama, as portrayed by Claudia McNeil, who had such an ability "to tweak the heartstrings," as one reviewer noted. Sydney Poitier as Walter Lee was "noble" and "heroic," and the entire ensemble "stunning."

Audiences watched a full evening of the heartbreaks and triumphs of a black family and when they left the theater they felt good—about themselves and about the world. They were surprised, and pleased, by their own reactions. Why, the Youngers were just like any other family! And Mama—wise, exasperating, loving—was just like their own sweet mothers. At first, Lorraine was delighted by the praise and attention, but she soon grew troubled. Many whites seemed to take these warm feelings as proof that they themselves were just fine, that, yes, there were mean people who would treat the Youngers badly, but that didn't include *them.* Why, not only had they enjoyed the play, but they'd actually identified with the characters—black characters! Didn't that make them less guilty of racial intolerance than most everyone else? Certainly

83

less than those terrible people on television, the ones who set dogs and firehoses on defenseless black people?

In an effort to recover *Raisin*'s original message—that all people, no matter how downtrodden, have within them "the very essence of human dignity," and to push the play's audience to understand the larger issues of racial justice, she decided to include major changes in the screenplay for the film version, which she had agreed to write. Random House wanted to publish the script later the same year, and Lorraine would insist they include the scenes and sections cut during the rehearsal period. These inclusions, she believed, would make the Youngers' ongoing struggle against racism all the more immediate and powerful. Lorraine also vowed to use the many interviews she granted to, in effect, plead the Youngers' case again. As she set to work, it almost seemed to Lorraine that after having seen her brilliant child through its birth, infancy, and childhood, now, just when she thought *A Raisin in the Sun* would stand on its own, it needed her more than ever.

NINE

The Goddess

INTERVIEWER: And what about success—this little goddess Success?

L.H.: I think it's wonderful, it's wonderful. . . . I'm enjoying every bit of it!

—Lorraine Hansberry,
To Be Young, Gifted, and Black

L ORRAINE HANSBERRY was the most talked-about young woman in all of New York City in the spring of 1959. To a reporter from *The New Yorker* magazine, she gushed about how often the phone rang and how every time she picked it up was an adventure. By May, she recounted, she'd already had the number changed several times, and just when she was sure it was truly secret, it would ring and the person on the other end would say, "This is So-and-So of the BBC!"

Lorraine went on to describe a typical day since fame had struck. The morning might start with a TV or radio interview, then on to a luncheon for a Negro professional organization, after which she'd hurry back to her Greenwich Village apartment to take Spice for a walk, and usually someone would be waiting for her in the lobby. Later she'd dress up for dinner and another reception which she'd attend with Bob, before coming home to eat banana cream pie ("I'm mad for banana cream pie!") and watch a TV show featuring the interview she'd given that morning. As she laughingly told a reporter, "What sort of happens is you just hear from everybody!" And she found "No" a nearly impossible reply to any request. Her plate was full. As Langston Hughes wrote in one of his poems, "Success"

> ...is a great big beefsteak
> with onions on it,
> and I eat.

Magazines and newspapers loved to talk about her unpretentious ordinariness, her "quite ramshackle" apartment, where there were records lying on the floor and even a dish full of pennies. Lorraine herself looked like a college girl in a "writing uniform" of white socks, sneakers, and chinos. This, they all loved to mention, despite the fact that *A Raisin in the Sun* was bringing her 10 percent of the weekly gross of $4,000, plus "a big whack" of the $300,000 that Columbia Pictures had paid for the movie in early 1960.

Only a few months after *Raisin*'s opening, Lorraine Hansberry received the prestigious New York Drama Critics' Circle Award for Best American play of 1959, beating out Tennessee Williams and Eugene O'Neill. She was clearly becoming a cultural icon. Her embrace by the theater world was not unlike Jackie Robinson's entry into previously all-white Major League baseball. It was more than mere recognition of a fresh young talent; she'd become a symbol of what seemed to be America's new social maturity about race issues.

All in all, she didn't mind if people talked about her as long as they listened, too. "People Are Talking About... LORRAINE HANSBERRY," proclaimed a headline in *Vogue Magazine,* May 1959. "Although caught up in the pounce of publicity, she has remained a quiet woman who lives three flights up in a Greenwich Village walkup...." Quiet? Lorraine thought to herself, hardly. In fact, if her fame meant anything, it offered her the chance to turn up the volume and air her concerns about race relations in the United States.

The comment came up over and over: "It seems from the enthusiastic reception by white audiences that this is not really a play about Negroes—it's a play about people— in fact, it could be about anybody." Lorraine would always respond as politely, but firmly, as possible. She knew that people expected a Negro play to be "different," to be a *thwump* on the back of the head, a propaganda piece. She would counter: "The emotions and feelings in *A Raisin in the Sun* may seem universal, but the setting and charactes are very specific.... It's not even a New York family or a southern Negro family. It is specifically South Side Chicago.... In other words, I think people, to the extent we accept them and believe them as who they're supposed to be, to that extent they become everybody."

Yet it seemed the more Lorraine talked about universal versus specific or realism versus naturalism, the more she was misunderstood and misinterpreted. In fact, it seemed when Lorraine Hansberry became someone whom "People Are Talking About"—that is, when she won the New York Drama Critics' Circle Award, received a Tony nomination, and signed the movie deal—she became more and more separated from her play. *A Raisin in the Sun* was in fact being taken from her, snatched away by high-minded critics, academics, and theatergoers, all of whom emerged from the Ethel Barrymore Theatre warmed by a comforting, self-congratulatory glow. If I identify so closely with characters so different from me, they were able to say to themselves, I must be more compassionate than I'm given credit for.

Lorraine was upset but not surprised at this turn of events. *Raisin* was a protest play, although the objects of the protest were the same people who applauded so enthusiastically each night. They watched sympathetically as Walter Lee lost the family's money and then discovered his own manhood. They were so happy that the Youngers could leave their cramped apartment and buy a new house in a white suburb. In this way, according to actor Ossie Davis, who replaced Sidney Poitier as Walter Lee Younger on Broadway, they managed to kidnap the play's message.

I should have known, Lorraine thought, as the play was passed from enthusiastic Broadway audiences to the critics and back again, twirling round and round, and on to Hollywood. When it finally emerged from this dance, it was hardly recognizable. It *was* the same play, but it had been molded to fit many different visions.

She couldn't help but think back to the experience of her own father twenty years before when, after winning his Supreme Court battle over restricted housing, he had returned to Chicago to find that nothing had changed and that blacks still couldn't live where they wanted to. Carl had moved to Mexico, "an embittered exile," as she described him. Lorraine, however, was younger, maybe stronger, and she resolved to fight back. During the weeks and months that followed *Raisin*'s initial media splash, she wrote countless letters to the editor and gave numerous speeches, and in each she tried to make clear who she really was and what her words meant.

She could not, for example, let stand the comments of *New York Times* reporter Nan Robertson who, in an article titled "Dramatist against Odds," quoted Lorraine as saying that *Raisin* wasn't a "negro play" but a play about "honest-to-god believable many-sided people who happen to be negroes." Lorraine clipped this article, pasted it in a scrapbook, and wrote next to it: "Never said NO SUCH THING." She immediately sent off a letter to the *Times* editor asking that Nan Robertson retract the statement, but she heard nothing and the letter was never published. Indeed, not only was the damage done, but the controversy seemed to grow beyond Lorraine's power to control. Within days she read that she, Lorraine Hansberry, didn't consider herself a Negro writer, but a "writer who happens to be negro."

At this same time, Lorraine was interviewed on television by reporter Mike Wallace, who brought up these very same quotes. Wasn't it true, he plunged in, that your play is a "success because it was a negro play written by a negro playwright?" Lorraine, by now, understood the tactic: attribute *Raisin*'s success to her own uniqueness, to the fact that she was different from others of her race. Then racism won't be the issue, it will be Lorraine Hansberry. When Mike Wallace asked why, given *Raisin's* acceptance and popularity, there were not more plays by blacks produced, Lorraine answered without hesitation: "Racial discrimination in the industry, of course."

Yet her letters, speeches, and interviews didn't attract the amount of attention that her "little play" did. *A Raisin in the Sun* had become a cultural phenomenon—a screen for people everywhere to find confirmation of their own beliefs and values. And the uncompromising sensibility of the 1960s, where left and right, good and bad, black and white were clearly delineated, left little hope that there would be a multivisioned interpretation of *Raisin's* message any time soon.

To make matters worse, just as it was becoming quite clear that whites were throwing a hood over *Raisin's* message, black academics and critics decided that the play's success with white audiences was proof that it was a "sell-out." Lorraine was being rejected as an "assimilationist," the same criticism Beneatha launches at Ruth and Walter Lee as they dance cheek-to-cheek to a sultry blues record. (Beneatha would have them performing a Nigerian folk dance instead.) "You seem to wish to quarrel with me about what you consider fuzzy-headed idealism," she wrote in a letter. "I absolutely plead guilty to the charge of idealism. But simple idealism. You see, our people don't really have a choice. We must come out of the ghettos of America, because the ghettos are killing us; not only our dreams, as Mama says, but our very bodies."

By 1960, Lorraine had begun to write the movie

screenplay for *A Raisin in the Sun*. She'd been promised at least some artistic control and so, as she settled down to work, she looked forward to expanding the play's original message. She wrote several new scenes which were all intended to underline not only the harsh living conditions, but the Younger family's feeling of entrapment. Lorraine's script called, for example, for Walter Lee, in his bright chauffeur's uniform, to hold the door open for his wealthy employer. Mama would battle with a store clerk over poor quality and high prices. Interestingly, too, Lorraine tilted the "main character" balance toward Walter Lee, as Sidney Poitier had battled for during the play's rehearsals. Yet in the end, only some of Lorraine's script changes were used in the film. The filmmaker's main guide seemed to be caution, inoffensiveness, and profitability.

The film version of *A Raisin in the Sun* was not considered an artistic success, although it did win a special humanitarian award at the 1961 Cannes Film Festival, and many people still consider the film immensely powerful. The movie, beautifully acted once again by the original Broadway cast, suffered from uninspired directing. Lorraine's script had called for several scenes to be shot outside of the apartment—on a street corner and at Mama's place of employment, for example—but Columbia Pictures wanted the film to be as much like the Broadway production as possible. According to Robert Nemiroff, the studio simply scrimped and saved, thinking there wasn't a big market for a film about black people. In the end, Lorraine was relieved the studio didn't make more changes to her screenplay.

By the summer of 1961, the hubbub over *Raisin* had settled enough so that Lorraine could return to work on other projects. She and Robert had no financial worries, but Lorraine felt worn and frazzled by the endless contentiousness. She saw Robert little, yet needed the solace of their loving partnership more than ever. She longed for solitude and a quiet place to work and so when she heard about a home for sale in Croton-on-Hudson, a quiet town about sixty minutes north of New York City, she hoped it would become a needed retreat for them both. The house was simple, modern, with huge glass windows looking out onto the quiet wooded countryside. There was a spacious lawn for Spice and their new dog, a German Shepherd puppy named Chaka. At the close of that year, Lorraine wrote to a friend that it had been "a raucous couple of years but now I am back to work here in the woods."

TEN

Is Anyone Listening?

INTERVIEWER: Miss Hansberry...What are your plans for the future? What do you work on next?

L.H.: I want to continue just tackling things and writing plays all the way out, and those that I think have some merit I will dare to read to other people, as I finally dared to read "the One."

—Lorraine Hansberry,
To Be Young, Gifted, and Black

DEEP IN THE sheltering woods of Croton-on-Hudson, Lorraine Hansberry worked on various projects that would expand on the themes she first tackled in *A Raisin in the Sun*. She kept a note on her writing table: *"PRO-POSED WORK—September 1960"* began the eclectic list, which included: *"The Sign in Jenny Reed's Window,* musical drama; *A Revolt of Lemmings,* novel; *The Life of Mary Wollstonecraft,* full-length drama (Thesis: Strong-minded woman of rationality; and a creature of history; nonetheless, a human being, destroyed many times over by 'life as she is lived'); *Les Blancs* (The Holy Ones); *The Drinking Gourd*, TV play—into stage play (?); some short stories . . . The Musical . . . ."

She hoped these works would help both clarify and indeed rescue her public persona. The last thing she wanted was to become, as her alter-ego Beneatha Younger might say, "an old-fashioned Negro." Lorraine's father had been an old-fashioned Negro—proper, meticulous, faithful to the tenets of American democracy—and yet it was, she believed, profound disappointment and disillusionment that had killed him.

Still, Lorraine allowed herself to be idealistic enough to believe *Raisin*'s success was a sign that after the stiflingly conformist years of the 1950s, Americans were "again ready to listen," as she told an interviewer. The fearsome atmosphere that had been created by Senator McCarthy and his House Un-American Activities Committee had given way to something hopeful. She longed to believe that *Raisin*'s diverse audience would stick by her and keep listening.

One of the projects Lorraine eagerly took on was a script for a television drama. It had been commissioned late in 1959 by television producer-director Dore Schary, "one of the more socially committed producers in Hollywood," according to Robert Nemiroff. Mr. Schary would produce the series for NBC, which was planning to commemorate the centennial of the Civil War with a series of five ninety-minute television dramas, each written by a major playwright of the day. The series would be, according to an early press release, "one of the most important events of coming TV seasons."

Lorraine's play, which would lead off the series, was to be about slavery. She looked upon this as an opportunity to get an important message across to millions of television viewers. She would be able to use her fame to give Americans a different look at a pivotal period in their history and especially at that "peculiar institution," slavery. Dore Schary assured Lorraine that she would feel no pressure from him, or from NBC, to make her work "acceptable." The script, he insisted, should be "as frank as it needs to be."

Yet shortly after giving Lorraine the go-ahead to pursue her subject wherever it led, Dore Schary met again with NBC executives. He was pleased to tell them that for the first script he'd commissioned the much talked-about young black woman who'd won the Drama Critics' Circle Award for best Broadway play. His announcement was greeted with a deafening silence. "What's her point of view about it—slavery?" someone asked. Mr. Schary, thinking this was an attempt at humor, answered with exaggerated seriousness. "She's against it," he replied. "Nobody laughed," he remembered later, "and I knew we were dead."

Lorraine knew nothing about NBC's ambivalence. Relieved to be away from the distractions of sudden stardom, she plunged into her research on slavery. For several months in early 1960, she spent long hours in the Main Reading Room of the New York Public Library as well as at the Schomburg Collection in Harlem. She pored over transcripts, speeches, diaries, and journals.

"We've been trying very hard in America," she said at the time, "to pretend that this greatest conflict didn't

97

even have at its base the only thing it did have at its base . . . ." Instead, everyone talked about cotton, tobacco, and the exalted Southern way of life—about, as Lorraine commented wryly, "beautiful ladies in big fat dresses screaming as their houses burned down from the terrible, nasty, awful Yankees." Yet what exactly was the "Southern way of life?" she wondered. It seemed so much easier to speak of the South in terms of "the economy" and ignore what propped it all up: unpaid labor, brutally and inhumanely maintained. Yet it was this horrific institution that allowed Southerners to prosper socially and economically.

The picture of slave life seen in popular novels like *Gone with the Wind* and even *Uncle Tom's Cabin* had been filtered through white people's eyes, and always looked nearly the same. First, there was Mammy, the erstwhile black Earth Mother, nurturing and disapproving. She seemed in her glory within a large family, either white or black. Prissy, the younger woman, was loud and silly and inept. These slaves always seemed so comfortable on the plantation, one could almost be convinced it *would* be cruel to take them away. Their lives were so orderly, so secure; the only thing missing, Lorraine noted, was their own humanity.

Still, as in all her work, Lorraine didn't want to just write a polemic tract. She wanted instead to lead her audience to a complex view of humanity so they could see that the problem was not simply with the institution of slavery but with the economy that relied on its injustices. "When the system is foul," she proclaimed, "everything else smells as well." She thought about her own grandmother, born into slavery, and her grandfather who snuck into the hills behind the plantation, leaving his family sick with worry.

In *The Drinking Gourd,* Lorraine introduces characters from two families: one a slave, and the other, a slave-owner. The main focus for each family is a rebellious son. In the aristocratic Sweet family, the patriarch Hiram, who is in poor health, agonizes over his mean-spirited, impulsive son Everett, who will one day take over the plantation. Everett constantly reminds his father that the farm will be much more profitable if he keeps his slaves in closer check, driving them harder and tolerating no appeals for sympathy.

Not surprisingly, Everett completely supports the cause of Southern independence. He is certain both that there will soon be a war and that the Confederate forces will whip the Union in a matter of a few weeks. Hiram dreads the coming conflict, an inevitable one in his view, and grieves for the impetuousness of Everett's generation. He worries, too, about the plantation's new overseer, hand-picked by Everett, who drives the slaves with an almost sadistic zeal.

One of the most influential of the Sweet's slaves is Rissa, the cook. She is very close to Hiram Sweet and has often appealed to him for help in matters concerning her own family. She tells him nothing, however, about the frequent disappearances of her son Hannibal. Hannibal has a taste for freedom and sneaks away to a clearing in a woods near the slave quarters. There he stares up at the stars, particularly the Big Dipper—the constellation the slaves call "The Drinking Gourd" which points north, toward freedom. There, too, he pulls the Sweet's family

Bible from his shirt and reads. "I kin read, Sarah," Hannibal says, and Sarah knows he is in real danger.

Rissa despairs over Hannibal's disappearances and goes into the woods at night to leave food for him. At the same time, she notices that as Hiram Sweet's health deteriorates, his mean-spirited son Everett is taking tighter control of the plantation. Rissa knows that young Mr. Sweet will not ignore what Hiram chooses to.

Hannibal is found out in the woods one night by Everett and Zeb, the plantation overseer. After Hannibal makes a futile attempt to escape, Everett orders Zeb to put Hannibal's eyes out: "As long as he can see, he can read," he explains. Hiram, who had prided himself on his benevolent rule of the plantation, is distressed by Hannibal's fate and asks Rissa to believe he had nothing to do with it. Rissa's pain, however, is too raw for forgiveness. "Ain't you *Marster*?" she asks, "How can a man be marster of some men and not at all of others?"

What is a master? Lorraine asks again, so many years after first pondering the question at her grandmother's knee. How can one be considered a master, and yet have no power over the evil in one's midst? Lorraine also challenged the comforting image of the Black Mammy, whose shadow crowded Mama in *A Raisin in the Sun.* Rissa, all loving and forgiving, finally loses her patience and turns on her master. She hears Hiram's cries for help as he lays dying outside her cabin yet, except for rocking slowly and steadily in her chair, she doesn't move.

"Apparently it was controversial," Lorraine told a symposium on the "Negro Writer in America," held on January 1, 1961. "When they asked for *The Drinking Gourd,* it was to have been the first of a special series for the Centennial by serious dramatists, but I'm afraid . . . they hadn't yet resolved who won the Civil War." The network executives squirmed. They worried about offending Southern viewers and making others uncomfortable. Lorraine, however, had been under the impression that *educating* viewers, especially Southern ones was, at least in part, the mission of the series.

Dore Schary read several drafts of the script at various stages and pronounced it "powerful. . . marvelous." Shortly after receiving the final version, he called Lorraine to say that Henry Fonda had agreed to play the soldier/narrator, and that the eminent British actor Laurence Olivier was considering the role of Hiram Sweet. The rest of the cast, Mr. Schary was certain, would be of similar quality. He added that NBC now had the script, and their reaction should be forthcoming.

Lorraine never heard directly from NBC. Instead, she read of *The Drinking Gourd*'s fate in the *New York Herald Tribune*. The headline read: "Dore Schary Tells Why TV Shies from Civil War," and the article contained an excerpt from an NBC press release which expressed network concerns about offending the South. Dore Schary's job itself fell victim to NBC's desire to be unobjectionable. After he had solicited five scripts from five dramatists and had cast the first of these, his contract was allowed to lapse. The other Civil War projects were quietly canceled. "They asked me for it," Lorraine told the symposium. "They paid me . . . attached a notation to it saying, moreover, that they thought it was 'superb' and then they put it in a drawer."

Lorraine couldn't help but feel stung by both the shabby treatment and the waste of time and energy. She wanted to stamp her feet and shout, "It's not fair!" but then realized that "fairness" was exactly the problem. *The Drinking Gourd*'s treatment of Hiram Sweet and Rissa, of Everett and Hannibal, had been too fair. Hiram was judicious and kind, yet he was powerless in the face of his own son's evil. Rissa was patient and forgiving, yet does nothing at the end when Hiram begs for help. These characters don't do what we want them to do: they go against our sense of the order of things. And who wants that?

"Ultimately," as she wrote in a letter to a young woman seeking advice about writing plays that would get produced, "the only answer to it is your own: To completely ignore all of it and write the best that one can about whatever matter agitates one, and try to strike art." She didn't pretend, however, that this was easy advice to follow. She longed for an easier time herself—self-discipline always bedeviled her—and sometimes even longed to relive the hectic whirlwind of 1959–1960, when she was too distracted by fame to worry about her own life.

What was the price of fame? Lorraine and Bobby bought the Croton house together, yet clearly it was meant to be Lorraine's house. She was to live there alone, something she'd tried her entire life to avoid, but now it was the only thing that made sense.

An air of mystery surrounds the breakup of Lorraine's and Bob's marriage, and perhaps about Lorraine's commitment to it all along. She and Bob were clearly soulmates and artistic partners. She relied on his strength, guidance, and devotion, all of which were crucial to her success. But what about romance? Years later, anonymous letters were discovered among Lorraine's papers, which had been written during the mid-1950s to a lesbian journal called *The Ladder*. In them, she discusses the role of women in conventional society and decries the fact that marriage is a woman's only alternative. Many have since come to believe that Lorraine might have been a lesbian whose marriage, while loving in a certain sense, was also a matter of convenience. For now, the real story remains private.

At her house in the woods, Lorraine struggled with the "utter aloneness" of her life. She admitted to herself that loneliness was another of her phobias—like flying, crossing bridges, or riding elevators. Yet here she was. "It really is better to be alone," she wrote in her journal, "horrible but better." When she wasn't writing, she played with Spice, her "almost collie," and trained her German Shepherd dog Chaka. She wrote long letters to friends, strangers, and many newspaper editors. She engaged in a long, memorable exchange with the novelist and controversial journalist Norman Mailer on the subject of his essay "The White Negro," published in 1957. On the surface, the essay was about blacks and hipness. Lorraine, like her friend James Baldwin, didn't think Norman Mailer knew much about the black experience and she told him so in the pages of the *Village Voice*.

Though she was actively engaged in getting her message across, she was physically isolated. "Blobbyglobby days again," she wrote in her journal. How she longed to be alone less often, to be surrounded by "a company of friends . . . laughters and dancers! We might do the Twist and then African and then Russian and laugh. . . . For money and fame I would make the exchange."

ELEVEN

Speaking for the Race

There is simply no reason why dreams should dry
up like raisins or prunes or anything else in
America. If you will permit me to say so, I believe
that we can impose beauty on our future....

—Lorraine Hansberry,
To Be Young, Gifted, and Black

As MUCH AS Lorraine hated being alone, she knew that
being around other people constantly was impossible as well. After the sudden success of *A Raisin in the Sun*
she had become, much to her surprise, a public figure.
James Baldwin, author of the groundbreaking novel *Go
Tell It on the Mountain,* remembered being with Lorraine
Hansberry in Philadelphia in 1959 when *Raisin* was in
tryouts. Never before, he recalled, had he seen so many
black people at the theater. After a performance one
night, he and Lorraine stood in the street behind the theater and suddenly a mob was all around them. "It only
happens once," Lorraine said happily, as she pulled a pen

out of her purse and began signing autographs. "I stood there and watched," James Baldwin remembered. "I watched the people, who loved Lorraine for what she had brought to them; and watched Lorraine, who loved the people for what they brought to her." She was wise enough, he added, "to recognize that black American artists are a very special case. One is not judged merely as an artist: the Black people crowding around Lorraine, whether or not they considered her an artist, assuredly considered her a witness. . . ."

Whites, and especially the white media, needed Lorraine Hansberry just as much as her black admirers did. The civil rights movement, young and innocent when Rosa Parks kept her seat on the Montgomery bus, was becoming larger and more insistent, and there were hints of something dangerous in the future. Lorraine Hansberry's *A Raisin in the Sun* had made difficult issues approachable, even uplifting. The white media wanted to believe she could do the same during these troublesome times. And Lorraine was willing to try.

Right from the start, young people inspired the decade of the 1960s, and nowhere was this more true than in the civil rights movement. When the decade began black college students, first in Greensboro, North Carolina, then in Nashville, Tennessee, and eventually throughout the South, began taking their seats at lunch counters and restaurants. Following the determined lead of Rosa Parks and Martin Luther King, Jr., these clean-scrubbed kids endured jeers and taunts. Their attackers, "normal white folks," poured ketchup on their clothes and crushed out cigarettes on their heads.

John F. Kennedy, the nation's youngest president, took office in 1961. In his inaugural address he asked young people to step forward and serve their country. Young black men and women continued to do just that as they peacefully, nonviolently, followed the rules of their movement, which included "Sit straight and always face the counter" and a reminder to be friendly and courteous. More and more students fell in step with the movement, marching, sitting-in, singing out. Students at Morehouse College in Atlanta took out a full-page ad in the city's newspapers. "An Appeal to Civil Rights," it stated: "Today's youth will not sit by submissively, while being denied all the rights, privileges, and joys of life."

Lorraine Hansberry, by virtue of her fame—her Broadway hit, the Drama Critics' Circle Award, her appearances on television and radio—was called upon to speak about these issues again and again. The white media especially turned to her for help sorting out the racial "problem," and she couldn't, nor did she want to, say no. She became involved in various civil rights organizations, including the newer, more radical, Student Nonviolent Coordinating Committee (SNCC, pronounced "Snick.")

SNCC was founded during a conference for nearly 200 "sit-in" leaders held at Shaw University in Raleigh, North Carolina, in April 1960. Martin Luther King, Jr. and other civil rights leaders also attended. The purposes of the gathering were to exchange stories, evaluate the present, and plan for the future. Before the weekend was over, however, the student leaders had seized attention from their elders and were insisting on more forceful action in several Deep South locations. They decided, for example, to send "field secretaries" into key cities to educate citizens about their rights, and to keep tabs on racial progress. The movement's so-called old guard, King's Southern Christian Leadership Conference and the NAACP, decried SNCC's tactics as too risky and potentially violent.

Another voice asking the student leaders to move cautiously was that of President Kennedy. He and his brother Attorney General Robert F. Kennedy were sympathetic to the goals of the civil rights movement, but also very sensitive to international front-page news stories about terror and violence in the Deep South. They found these headlines both embarrassing and distracting and wanted the movement's leaders to avoid violence if they could. The Attorney General urged SNCC, for example, to concentrate its efforts on voter registration and to not push for more general desegregation, especially in parts of Alabama and Mississippi. SNCC leaders, many of whom had been Freedom Riders—those who in 1960 and 1961 rode buses throughout the South to force integration of bus terminals—smelled high-level bribery. They hadn't come all this way, they argued, to take the easy way out; their commitment went beyond "good press."

"You asked me for my views of the 'Negro Question' in the United States," Lorraine began a letter to a young Southern white man, who wrote asking for her assessment of the factions in the civil rights movement. "Please understand that I do not mean that Dr. King or any of his associates are less than sincere in lifting the banner of love and nonviolence into the winds of the struggle. . . . At the same time . . . I have no illusion that it is enough . . . ." She, too, was increasingly disillusioned with the movement's reliance on peaceful assembly and on the courts to push through social change. The hollowness of Carl Hansberry's legal victories had taught her that "justice" is not just about laws; it can only accompany sweeping societal change. Was it possible, she wondered, that the victories claimed by civil rights activists were only a few symbolic acts meant to obscure the lack of real change? "In the twentieth century, men everywhere like to breathe," Lorraine wrote in a letter. "And the Negro citizen still cannot, you see, *breathe*. . . ."

As the decade of the 1960s progressed, she had to admit that her own idealism, her fervent hope that everyone could learn to live together, might be outdated. She began to sympathize with some of the most militant black activists, including Malcolm X. She had known about his work since 1954, when they were both journalists in Harlem—she was writing for *Freedom,* and he for *Muhammed Speaks,* his own Black Muslim newspaper. *Muhammed Speaks* advocated black separatism, a view which Lorraine found abhorrent. Now Malcolm X was a leader in his own right, snapping at the heels of Martin Luther King, Jr. and his Southern Christian Leadership Conference. Malcolm criticized nonviolence and compared the civil rights leaders to "professional beggars." Malcolm also was one of the first to move the discussion of racism from the South to the urban North—to New York, Philadelphia, Chicago—where ghetto conditions and police brutality were part of everyday life. Lorraine was increasingly intrigued.

On May 24, 1963, anger—her own and that of several other prominent blacks—finally spilled over at one fateful gathering, "the most dramatic meeting I have ever attended," according to one of the participants. It was held at the New York City apartment of Attorney General Robert F. Kennedy, and had been planned only the day before by Kennedy and James Baldwin. The two had met for breakfast to discuss the increasingly ominous racial climate in various Northern cities, including Chicago, Detroit, and New York. Kennedy wanted to know, for example, more about the Black Muslim movement and Malcolm X, about the housing crisis in Chicago, and which black voices, beyond those of politicians, black people listened to. As their breakfast drew to a close James Baldwin suggested that if they could meet again the next day, he would bring some friends to broaden the discussion.

On one day's notice, James Baldwin called one or two prominent policy experts, plus numerous artists, including singer and actress Lena Horne, Harry Belafonte, and Lorraine Hansberry. Kennedy came to the meeting with Burke Marshall, chief of the Civil Rights Division of the Justice Department. The two believed they enjoyed a special relationship with blacks and they had high hopes for making some progress. They envisioned the morning as a calm exchange of ideas and suggestions which would further the aims of both sides.

The meeting, however, got off to a bad start and only got worse. James Baldwin had asked a civil rights activist named Jerome Smith, a former Freedom Rider, to be the centerpiece of the meeting. Smith began by telling Kennedy that he found the need for such a meeting nauseating, a suggestion the Attorney General seemed to take personally. When a member of Kennedy's staff began to list some encouraging statistics, Smith cut in: "Okay, let's cut through the bull ... :" Robert Kennedy, visibly offended, turned away from Jerome Smith which provoked the others to take Smith's side and become increasingly confrontative. "You've got a great many very, very accomplished people in this room, Mr. Attorney General," Lorraine jumped in to say, "but the only man who should be listened to is that man over there. That is the voice of 22 million people."

Lorraine's comment led Jerome Smith to speak about his experiences with the civil rights movement in the South and his growing disillusionment with Martin Luther King, Jr.'s ideals of nonviolence. He further added that he could imagine one day picking up a gun to defend himself. He spoke with anger, impatience, and eloquence, and the Attorney General seemed to take on a sullen dislike for him.

"Look," Lorraine added, "if you can't understand what this young man is saying then we are without any hope at all because you and your brother are representatives of the best that a white America can offer; and if you are insensitive to this, then there's no alternative except our going in the streets."

Robert Kennedy and his aides had no idea what had gone wrong or how to get the meeting back on track. The more the Attorney General struggled to bring the discussion back to a mutual exchange, as he'd originally envisioned it, the more it went off course. At one point, he began to talk about the plight of Irish immigrants in the nineteenth century and how his own family had overcome discrimination. Perhaps black people could do the same thing, he suggested.

"You do not understand at all," Baldwin jumped in. "Your grandfather came as an immigrant from Ireland and your brother is president of the United States .... My ancestors came to this country in chains, as slaves." The rest of the blacks pressed on, determined to get one message across: The government must take immediate action to ensure equality. Soon the "discussion" became "emotional verbal assaults," as one of the participants recalled. Kennedy himself said of the meeting: "They seemed possessed. They reacted as a unit. It was impossible to make contact with any of them."

Kennedy eventually stopped speaking altogether, and the meeting collapsed. Lorraine Hansberry was the first to leave the apartment but the others followed shortly afterwards. The disastrous encounter seemed to have hardened both sides. The Attorney General thought his brother's administration deserved more credit than they'd been given by this "uppity" group. James Baldwin's friends, including Lorraine, were confirmed in their beliefs that white liberals like Robert F. Kennedy were too sheltered by power and privilege to understand them.

One of the oddities of the occasion was that the Attorney General chose to meet with only a few policy experts, but many artists. Would he have met with white artists to discuss the white urban poor? How often does it happen that a black writer is regarded as an expert in all matters pertaining to black people? James Baldwin had asserted that "black American artists are a very special case," not just artists but witnesses as well. The challenge, however, for Lorraine, as well as for others thrust into this position, would be to find the right balance between art and political activism.

"Tuesday, had some weird attack," she began a journal entry that same spring. "Almost conked out. Went to Dr. on Wednesday. Results: Sick girl . . . ." The dizzy spells sent her to the doctor, who diagnosed a stomach ulcer and anemia and prescribed bed rest so she could regain her strength. Her illness, which came on so suddenly and sapped her energy so completely, caused her to consider her life's choices. Later that year she wrote in her journal that perhaps it was time to decide between social activism or artistic commitment, play-writing over witnessing: "I sit at this desk for hours," she wrote, "and sharpen pencils and smoke cigarettes and switch from play to play—Sidney, Toussaint, *Les Blancs* and—nothing happens. I begin to think more and more of doing something else with my life while I am still young. I mean almost anything—driving an ambulance in Angola or running a ski lodge in upstate NY—instead of this endless struggle. I expect the theater would kill me. . . ."

TWELVE

It's about Commitment

I care. I care about it all. It takes too much energy
not to care. Yesterday I counted twenty-six gray
hairs on the top of my head all from trying *not* to
care.

—Lorraine Hansberry,
The Sign in Sidney Brustein's Window

Lorraine Hansberry cared deeply—about her work, her
people, her society. Yet she couldn't help but look
around her and wonder, at this crucial time in American
history, was it possible commitment was waning? Of
course, there were examples of great bravery—such as
the Freedom Riders, who risked their lives to register
Southern blacks to vote—yet those seemed oddly isolated. White liberal intellectuals like her former
Greenwich Village neighbors, who might have been join-
ing the struggle for peace and justice, were instead afloat
in a sea of fashionable despair.

Despair, Lorraine believed, was available only to the

comfortable and secure. Its close kin, victimhood, was something to struggle against, like racism and war. As Lorraine wrote *The Sign in Sidney Brustein's* [formerly *Jenny Reed's*] *Window,* her second full-length play, it was therefore fitting that she dedicated it to "the committed everywhere." Commitment, Lorraine believed, was not just a cause or an issue, but the true purpose of art. Yet she knew that such a notion belonged more to her father's generation than her own. Most of her peers in the theater would certainly consider her quaint and old-fashioned.

Meanwhile, during the summer of 1963 her doctor ordered more tests. He suspected cancer of the intestinal tract but wouldn't know without exploratory surgery. Lorraine called her mother, who now lived in California. (The family business, Hansberry Enterprises, had recently failed.) Nannie and Mamie flew to New York to be with Lorraine, who was terrified of hospitals and everything to do with *real* illness.

The surgery proved the diagnosis correct, but Lorraine's doctor was confident that the cancerous tissue had been completely removed. Lorraine returned home to Croton and did, for a while, feel better. That summer, she presided over a gathering at a synagogue in Croton-on-Hudson, speaking along with Jerome Smith, who had spoken so movingly to Robert Kennedy about his experiences in the South. After the speeches, funds were sought and enough money was collected to buy a station wagon, which would carry civil rights workers to Mississippi where they would help poor blacks register to vote.

Her health prevented her from attending the now-famous March on Washington, held on August 28, 1963.

While 250,000 black and white people listened to Martin Luther King, Jr. deliver his "I Have a Dream" speech next to the Washington Monument, Lorraine prepared to go to Boston for another round of surgery. The winds blowing from the capitol that year seemed more hopeful than Lorraine's own fortunes.

That fall, however, the talk was of murder and death. In September, in Birmingham, Alabama, four little girls, attending church in frilly dresses and hats, were killed instantly when a bomb exploded. Two months later, on November 22, President Kennedy was shot and killed. The nation seemed to withdraw into a kind of grim introspection.

By January 1, 1964, Lorraine was happy to tell her journal that, "The work goes superbly! Yes: Sidney Brustein!" She was weak from her illness and its treatment, but she forced herself to concentrate her energy on one project. The play that had been *The Sign in Jenny Reed's Window* now belonged to Sidney Brustein. It would be her final message to the world, and she was ready to pour the last of her strength into it. "Only death can stop me now. . . ." she wrote in her journal.

As the play begins, Sidney Brustein is carrying out shelving from his failed nightclub. He's tired and discouraged. We soon learn—even before his wife, Iris—that he's now bought a newspaper publishing enterprise, yet this new undertaking doesn't excite him much. When a friend approaches him on behalf of a political candidate whom he hopes the newspaper will endorse, Sidney states unequivocally, "My little artsy-craftsy newspaper is going to stay clear of politics. Any kind of politics." He doesn't happen to have those kind of interests anymore.

By the next scene, however, Sidney has reconsidered his apolitical stance. His friend has not only convinced Sidney to endorse his candidate but to hang a sign in his window as well. The sign reads: "CLEAN UP COMMUNITY POLITICS: Wipe out Bossism VOTE REFORM."

The sign hangs there, throughout the play, as a testimonial to what is missing from the lives of Sidney, his wife Iris, and the rest of the people who walk in and out of their Greenwich Village living room. It is, in a word, "commitment." Sidney's and Iris' marriage flounders; Iris, who talks often of becoming an actress, can never make it to an audition. The other characters come and go from the Brustein living room, talking of psychoanalysis, Jewishness, homosexuality, and a whole range of other subjects. Yet, every topic seems to lead back to the speaker and his or her diminished capacity for concern and care. As Sidney says, "I no longer really believe that spring will come at all."

Proof that truly committed activists can't afford such indulgence came that summer from the deepest South. In June, the station wagon purchased after the Croton meeting carried three civil rights workers to Mississippi to help with a voter registration drive. It was dangerous work, Lorraine admitted, as she noted in her journal on July 17: "I think when I get my health back I shall go into the South to find out what kind of revolutionary I am...." Just outside of Philadelphia, Mississippi, Andrew Goodman, Michael Schwerner, and James Chaney were pulled over by local deputies. They were never seen alive again.

In August, their bodies were found in the Tallahaga River.

As Lorraine went back and forth to Boston that same summer for radiation treatment, she continued revising her play. She also wrote the text for a photo-documentary of the civil rights movement, called simply *The Movement.* Back in New York, she learned that the three producers of *The Sign on Sidney Brustein's Window* had secured financing and set the opening for October 1964. The cast was assembled and ready to begin rehearsal. One of the producers was Robert Nemiroff, from whom Lorraine was very quietly divorced. They told only family and close friends. Many only learned later, and never understood the reasons for the timing. Lorraine was very ill, gravely perhaps: Why divorce now? The two remained close working partners, however, and she relied on him throughout her illness.

In late September, Lorraine and a private nurse moved into the Hotel Abbey Victoria on Seventh Avenue so that Lorraine could be near the Longacre Theater, where *The Sign in Sidney Brustein's Window* was scheduled to open on October 15. Lorraine attended many of the rehearsals, often in a wheelchair and in great pain. She still hadn't been told that her illness was fatal and, on her good days, was convinced she would regain her full strength.

When the play opened on Wednesday evening, everyone involved knew Lorraine was weakening. Robert Nemiroff hoped the New York critics' reception would boost her spirits, if not her health. "Whatever the outcome tonight, I want you to know," he wrote in an opening-night telegram: "If the sign hangs long in the window, it is your sign.... You are tough, Lorraine Hansberry...even wracked with pain as now.... You are the best that we have. Good health, justice tonight, and more to come."

Some of the reviews glowed with praise. One, in Thursday's *New York Times,* said the characters "shine with humor, tremble with feeling and summon up a vision of wisdom and integrity." Others, however, saw it differently: "I would prefer not to cause her further pain. But the play is dreadful," wrote a critic in the *Village Voice.* Still others were simply puzzled: Why, given Lorraine's unique artistic vision and her insight into the lives of black people, did she write her second full-length play about white intellectuals? Why, at a time when black leaders like Malcolm X questioned the very concept of racial integration, did Lorraine Hansberry decide that race doesn't matter? Robert Nemiroff and the other producers knew as soon as they saw the early reviews that the play was in trouble. It was not, he noted later, because there were a few bad ones, but that the critics had completely misunderstood the play's message. And if they didn't get it, how could they encourage the theatergoing public to give it a chance?

The economics of Broadway dictated that if Lorraine's play wasn't either an unqualified hit, a musical, or had a big star leading the cast, it would not be able to sell enough advance tickets to stay open. It cost $20,000 to keep *Sidney Brustein* at the Longacre Theater for one week. Robert did the math and realized the play would need to close, not just soon, but after Saturday's performance, after less than a week's run. Now he had to break the news to Lorraine.

That Friday morning, the producers visited Lorraine at her hotel room and told her the play would close the next day. She was disappointed but not entirely surprised. She'd always seen her commercial success as a happy accident and not something to take for granted. Success like that was, she knew, serendipitous. Others more worthy— she thought of her old friend Langston Hughes—were often passed over to satisfy the public's whims.

Yet, even someone as tough as Lorraine had trouble accepting how fast *Sidney* was coming to an end. It had needed just as many hours of devotion as *A Raisin in the Sun*, yet "the One" had run on Broadway for nineteen months. Robert's heart fell when Lorraine's wide eyes looked up and asked how she would now manage. What would happen if she couldn't work anymore? If she became too sick to write?

Before she became too lost in worry, Eleanor and Frank Perry, who codirected the groundbreaking film *David and Lisa*, stopped by the theater to contribute $2,500 toward keeping *Sidney* alive. Later that day other donations came in. The closing notice had already been posted at the theater, yet now it seemed, miraculously, there was a slight chance the play would stay open.

At noon the next day, Lorraine called Robert from her hotel, panic-stricken. She'd lost her sight and her entire lower body from her legs to her chest had become numb. She couldn't move. Robert sent a doctor and a nurse and later Lorraine was taken to the hospital.

The push to keep *Sidney* on Broadway took on a new urgency. Contributions came from the theater community and the play's own crew. When the producers had enough money for one more week, they removed the closing notice from the door and let the public know the box office was open once again. Lorraine, in her hospital room, greeted the news with "a great beaming smile." The next day, Sunday, she felt well enough to write to an old friend, "I often feel that everything in the world which can happen has happened to me .... I hope that you and Polly get in to see the show. It's ever so much more entertaining than the reviewers try to let on. *And it's very funny.*" She ended the letter there and never finished it. Quite possibly, Robert wrote, that was the last time she put words to paper. He thought it fitting that it would be to talk about the humor of her work, the part that gave her more pleasure than all the rest and which was often overlooked in the search for serious meaning.

As word of *Sidney*'s, and Lorraine Hansberry's, fate spread, many actors, directors, and writers offered their help. On Tuesday, October 20, not quite a week after opening night, Lorraine fell into a coma. Her doctor believed she could die in a few hours. Her mother and sister flew in from California and began a hospital vigil. When they were all together, the Hansberry family agreed to release the news of her condition. There seemed, as Robert remembered, no reason to hold anything back.

Old friends, actors and actresses, directors, producers, writers, stepped forward to promote the play on radio and television. Then, late in October, several people gathered at Eleanor and Frank Perry's New York apartment to map out a plan for *Sidney*'s survival. The group consisted mainly of New York artists and theater people, except for one man, Jerome Smith, who was in New York briefly before returning to his job as a CORE organizer in the South. "Two years ago," he began softly, "I first met Lorraine Hansberry—like many of the young people of the movement, I had come to enlist her support." He movingly described how she had influenced his life, opened up a world not just of political activism but of literature and ideas as well.

Those who attended Tuesday's meeting agreed to take out an ad in the *New York Times:* "An open letter," it began. "First-Rate Theatre Belongs on Broadway.... Miss Hansberry's new play is a work of distinction ... powerful, tender, moving, and hilarious.... We the undersigned ... urge you to see it *now.*" It was signed by leading members of the arts community, including James Baldwin, Ossie Davis, Ruby Dee, and playwright Lillian Hellman. The response, Robert Nemiroff remembered, was "rather like the bursting of a dam."

Lorraine's condition improved somewhat in November. She awoke from her coma to see her mother, sister, and Robert standing beside her. A few days later, her dear Uncle William Leo Hansberry visited her hospital room. He spoke about developments in Africa, including the newly independent nation of Kenya. Her spirits brightened visibly as her father's brother held her hand and chatted.

The Sign in Sidney Brustein's Window ran through Thanksgiving and then, finally, Robert decided the time had come to close. The last day was to be the last Sunday of November. At the end of that matinee, however, as the audience applauded enthusiastically, Ossie Davis, playwright and actor, who had followed Sidney Poitier in the role of Walter Lee Younger, stepped forward to urge the audience to do something about "the crisis at hand."

The audience seemed to lunge for the stage, forming lines to donate. "A collection desk was set up on the stage," a *Newsday* article described. "As the audience filed forward, actress Madeline Sherwood . . . shouted from the stage: 'This is the most exciting thing I've seen in New York." Five thousand dollars was donated on that day alone. It seemed the sign would hang in Sidney Brustein's window a bit longer.

The play enjoyed full houses through December. On December 31, Robert's and Lorraine's family toasted in the New Year in her hospital room. Lorraine, however, couldn't agree that there seemed to be anything "happy" about 1965. Less than two weeks later, on January 12, 1965, she woke up smiling and talkative, but then drifted into unconsciousness. At approximately 9:00 A.M., Lorraine was dead of cancer at the age of thirty-four. When the news spread, the decision was made to close *Sidney* forever, after 101 performances.

The funeral was held three days later, on January 15, in a blinding blizzard. Six hundred people—artists, civil rights activists, friends, family—crowded into a small, red-brick Harlem church. The Reverend Eugene Callender read messages from James Baldwin and Martin Luther King, Jr., and gave the eulogy. Then Paul Robeson, who had towered over Lorraine when she first met him at her father's house so many years ago, recited several verses of Negro folksongs and spoke briefly: "Her roots were deep in her people . . . . As Lorraine says farewell, she bids us to keep our heads high and to hold onto our strength and powers, to soar like the eagle."

Lorraine's body was taken home to snow-covered Croton-on-Hudson later that day. On her tombstone are inscribed lines from *The Sign on Sidney Brustein's Window* which speak of her life, her work, and the extraordinary three-month period where her own life, and that of her play, hung in the balance, together.

> I care. I care about it all. It takes too much energy *not* to care.... The why of why we are here is an intrigue for adolescents; the how is what must command the living. Which is why I have lately become an insurgent again.

THIRTEEN

Legacy

> Though it be a thrilling and marvelous thing to be
> merely young and gifted in such times, it is doubly
> so, doubly dynamic—to be young, gifted, and
> black. Look at the world that awaits you!
>
> —Lorraine Hansberry,
> *To Be Young, Gifted, and Black*

Lorraine Hansberry showed us, as one critic noted, that a good old-fashioned play is worth having around. Unfortunately, in the world of the 1960s, "good old-fashioned" anything was out of favor, and during the years following Lorraine's death both black and white critics took issue with her generous, universal approach to both art and politics. How could she, for example, a so-called black radical, write her last full-length play about white intellectuals?

Black nationalists and members of the Black Arts Movement viewed her as entirely too much of an integrationist. They'd given up on the nonviolence and compassion of

Martin Luther King, Jr. and "his" civil rights movement, and had embraced instead Malcolm X's call for racial separatism. Yet such critics didn't realize that Lorraine herself often defended Malcolm X to her white friends, or that he was among the mourners at her funeral on January 16, 1965, just a month before his own death.

Eventually, audiences, students, and critics alike were encouraged to take another look at her art and her life. Renewed interest in Lorraine Hansberry's work came about largely due to the efforts of her literary executor and former husband, Robert Nemiroff. Robert combed Lorraine's journals and sketches and in 1969 published an "informal autobiography" called *To Be Young, Gifted, and Black*. The title was taken from a speech given to the United Negro College Fund composition contest, which she judged.

Robert Nemiroff also wrote and produced a musical version of *A Raisin in the Sun,* called simply *Raisin,* which was produced on Broadway during 1974. It won the prestigious Tony Award that year for Best Musical. Still, Robert Nemiroff has been criticized for remaking Lorraine's work and for writing *To Be Young, Gifted, and Black* in a style that was not Lorraine's. On the other hand, the amount of work Lorraine Hansberry actually completed during her all-too-brief lifetime was limited, and Robert Nemiroff's efforts have helped to keep her name alive.

In 1984, the twenty-fifth anniversary of *A Raisin in the Sun*'s Broadway opening brought several revivals—including one at Washington's Kennedy Center—and new reviews and commentary. In a new introduction to the play, poet Amiki Baraka, who in 1960 had accused Lorraine of selling out to whites, wrote frankly: "We missed the essence of the work.... The play is an accurate telling and stunning vision of the real struggle." Film director Spike Lee, too young to have seen *A Raisin in the Sun* in 1959, noted that in the 1990s the play is "still fresh, it's still relevant. Lorraine Hansberry is a visionary."

On February 4, 1996, a gala evening, called simply "A Celebration of Lorraine Hansberry," was held at New York's Majestic Theater. The event was sponsored by the Schomburg Center for Research in Black Culture, a research unit of the New York Public Library; many luminaries, including Nobel Prize-winning author Toni Morrison, Harry Belafonte, and Ruby Dee, helped in the planning. Scenes from Lorraine's plays were staged and excerpts from filmed interviews were shown on a large screen. Then various artists and public figures spoke about Lorraine's enormous influence on those who followed. "She wrote about the black struggle for democracy in a language of thrilling ideas. She wrote about ideology as real life," said Amiki Baraka. "Writers live on that fine line between insanity and Jesus," said poet Nikki Giovanni. "If you want to tell the truth, you have to pick up your pen and take your chances. She made it possible for all of us to look a little deeper."

Chronology

1930   Lorraine Vivian Hansberry is born to Nannie
Perry Hansberry and Carl Augustus Hansberry
in Chicago, May 19.

1935   Lorraine is given a white fur coat for
Christmas. She's beaten up by her classmates
when she wears it to school in January 1936.

1938   The Hansberrys buy a home in a white neighborhood in Chicago. Neighbors throw bricks,
one narrowly missing Lorraine as she stands in
her living room. Carl is in Washington, D.C.,
fighting a legal battle against housing discrimination. Nannie takes the children to her
mother's home in Tennessee later that summer.

1940   Carl Hansberry and the NAACP win the landmark Supreme Court battle in the case
Hansberry v. Lee.

1944– Lorraine attends Chicago's Englewood High.
1948   School. During her freshman year, she wins a
coveted creative writing award. The Hansberry

home is the gathering spot for many leading black figures, including Langston Hughes, W. E. B. DuBois, Duke Ellington, and Paul Robeson.

1946   Carl Hansberry dies of a cerebral hemorrhage in Mexico, where he has retired.

1948– Lorraine graduates from Englewood in
1949   January. In February, she enters the University of Wisconsin at Madison. Politics and theater capture her interest.

1950   Lorraine leaves the university in February. Moves to New York City in the fall. Writes for *Young Progressives of America* magazine.

1951   Lorraine begins to work full-time for *Freedom* magazine. Meets Robert Nemiroff on a picket line.

1952   Lorraine is named *Freedom's* associate editor. Delivers a speech in Montevideo, Uruguay, for Paul Robeson, whose passport has been re-voked.

1953   Lorraine marries Robert Nemiroff on June 20 in Chicago. Resigns as *Freedom* editor but con-tinues as a contributor.

1956   Robert Nemiroff's song "Cindy, Oh, Cindy" is released and becomes a hit. Lorraine now be-gins to write full-time, concentrating on a play which she calls *The Crystal Stair*.

1957   Lorraine reads her first draft of *A Raisin in the Sun* aloud to several people gathered at her apartment. They decide to try to produce it for Broadway.

1959   *A Raisin in the Sun* is in tryouts in New Haven, Philadelphia, and Chicago. Opens March 11 to wide acclaim on Broadway. Receives the prestigious New York Drama Critics' Circle Award for Best American Play on May 4. Lorraine is commissioned by NBC to write *The Drinking Gourd* for the commemoration of the Civil War centennial. Also begins writing the film version of *A Raisin in the Sun*.

1960   Screenplay of *A Raisin in the Sun* and script of *The Drinking Gourd* are completed. Lorraine begins work on new plays: *Les Blancs* and *The Sign in [Jenny Reed's] Sidney Brustein's Window.*

1961   The film version of *A Raisin in the Sun* opens to mixed reviews. Wins award at Cannes Film Festival.

1962   During the summer, Lorraine and Robert move to Croton-on-Hudson. Lorraine is increasingly involved in civil rights organizing and fundraising. Later that year, she and Robert separate and he returns to New York City. Lorraine writes *What Use Are Flowers?* about nuclear winter. Revises *Les Blancs,* a play set in colonial Africa.

1963   Lorraine becomes ill in April. Together with other black leaders, she meets with Attorney General Robert F. Kennedy on May 24. Cancer of the duodenum diagnosed in June. Surgery in Boston in August.

1964	Lorraine is divorced from Robert on March 10. In September, she names Robert her literary executor. Writes text for *The Movement. The Sign in Sidney Brustein's Window* opens on Broadway, October 15.
1965	Lorraine Hansberry dies on January 12. *The Sign in Sidney Brustein's Window* closes on the same day. Funeral in Harlem, January 15.
1966	Nannie Perry Hansberry dies in Los Angeles.
1969	*To Be Young, Gifted, and Black,* produced by Robert Nemiroff, opens in New York. Companion book is published.
1970	Lorraine's unfinished play, *Les Blancs,* completed by Robert Nemiroff, opens on Broadway.
1970– 1972	*To Be Young, Gifted, and Black* tours the United States.
1973	Robert Nemiroff produces a musical version of *A Raisin in the Sun.* Called *Raisin,* it wins the Tony Award for best Broadway musical.
1989	Twenty-fifth anniversary of *A Raisin in the Sun*'s opening is marked by several new productions of the play, including *American Playhouse*'s uncut television version starring Danny Glover and Esther Rolle.

Selected Bibliography

Bigsby, C. W. E. *Modern American Drama, 1945–1990.* Cambridge: Cambridge University Press, 1992.

Bond, Jean Garey, ed. "Lorraine Hansberry: Art of Thunder, Vision of Light," *Freedomways 19* (4th Quarter, 1979).

Carter, Steven R. *Hansberry's Drama: Commitment amid Complexity.* Urbana and Chicago: University of Illinois Press, 1991.

Cheney, Anne. *Lorraine Hansberry.* New York: Twayne Publishers/Twayne's United States Author Series, 1994.

Duberman, Martin Bauml. *Paul Robeson.* New York: Alfred A. Knopf, 1988.

Grossman, James R. *Land of Hope: Chicago, Black Southerners, and the Great Migration.* Chicago: University of Chicago Press, 1989.

Hansberry, Lorraine. *The Collected Last Plays of Lorraine Hansberry.* Edited by Robert Nemiroff; foreword and afterword by Julius Lester; introduction by Margaret B. Wilkerson. New York: New American Library, 1983.

————. *Les Blancs: The Collected Last Plays*. Edited with critical background by Robert Nemiroff; introduction by Margaret B. Wilkerson. New York: Vintage Books, 1994.

————. *A Raisin in the Sun*. New York: The Modern Library, 1995.

————. *A Raisin in the Sun/The Sign in Sidney Brustein's Window*. Introduction by Robert Nemiroff; critical essays by Amiki Baraka and Frank Rich. New York: Vintage Books, 1995.

————. *A Raisin in the Sun: The Unfilmed Original Screenplay*. Introduction by Margaret B. Wilkerson; commentary by Spike Lee. New York: Signet/Penguin, 1994.

Hine, Darlene Clark, ed. *Black Women in America, Vol. 2*. Brooklyn, NY: Carlson Publishing, 1993.

Holli, Melvin G., and Peter d'A. Jones, eds. *The Ethnic Frontier: Group Survival in Chicago and the Midwest*. Grand Rapids, MI: William B. Eerdmans, 1977.

Keppel, Ben. *The Work of Democracy: Ralph Bunche, Kenneth B. Clark, Lorraine Hansberry and the Cultural Politics of Race*. Cambridge, MA: Harvard University Press, 1995.

Lemann, Nicholas. *The Promised Land: The Great Black Migration and How It Changed America*. New York: Vintage Books, 1991.

McKissack, Patricia C., and Frederick L. McKissack. *Young, Black, and Determined: A Biography of Lorraine Hansberry*. New York: Holiday House, 1998.

Nemiroff, Robert. *To Be Young, Gifted, and Black: Lorraine Hansberry in Her Own Words*. With drawings and art by Lorraine Hansberry. New York: Vintage Books, 1995.

"People Are Talking About...," *Vogue* (July 1959), pp. 78–79.

Poitier, Sidney. *This Life*. New York: Alfred A. Knopf, 1980.

Rampersad, Arnold. "I Dream A World," *The Life of Langston Hughes, Vol. II: 1941–1967.* New York: Oxford University Press, 1988.

Spear, Allan H. *Black Chicago: The Making of a Negro Ghetto: 1890–1920*. Chicago: University of Chicago Press, 1967.

"Talk of the Town," *The New Yorker* (May 9, 1959), pp. 33–35.

Weatherby, W. J. *James Baldwin: Artist on Fire*. New York: Donald I. Fine, Inc., 1989.

Wilkerson, Margaret B. "Sighted Eyes And Feeling Heart of Lorraine Hansberry," *Black American Lit. Forum* 17 (1982): 8–14.

Young, Brenda Joyce. "Baldwin and Hansberry as 'Privileged Speakers': Two Black Writers and the Civil Rights Movement, 1955–1965." Unpublished Ph.D. dissertation, Emory University, 1996.

Index

139

INDEX

Acknowledgments

Thanks to Cathy Gourley, former editor of the Barnard Biography Series, for calling me out of the blue one day about this assignment. She gave me invaluable support and advice about the early chapters, even after she'd moved on to other projects. Claudia Schaab at Conari Press was wonderful at gently coaxing more research, more thinking, more *words*. I also appreciate the assistance of the research staff at the Schomburg Center for Research in Black Culture, The New York Public Library, the Chicago Historical Society, the University of Wisconsin, Madison, the University of New Hampshire, and everyone at the Portsmouth Public Library, Portsmouth, New Hampshire, but especially Kate Giordano, who never met a title she couldn't get into her hands. I'm very grateful to Chiz Schultz for sharing his heartfelt memories of Robert Nemiroff. Thanks again to Charnan for taking me on a wild Lorraine Hansberry tour of Chicago. And, of course, love to J, N, and L, and thanks for putting up with all the crabby days.

About the Author

Susan Sinnott has written numerous books for children and teenagers, including biographies of Jacques Cousteau and three of the United States First Ladies. Her *Extraordinary Hispanic Americans* was named ALA's Best Reference Book of 1991. Sinnott resides in Eliot, Maine, and is currently working on two books for the American Girl Collection.

THE BARNARD BIOGRAPHY SERIES

The Barnard Biography series expands the universe of heroic women with these profiles. The details of each woman's life may vary, but each was led by a bold spirit and an active intellect to engage her particular world. All have left inspiring legacies that are captured in these biographies.

Barnard College is a selective, independent liberal arts college for women affiliated with Columbia University and located in New York City. Founded in 1889, it was among the pioneers in the crusade to make higher education available to young women. Over the years, its alumnae have become leaders in the fields of public affairs, the arts, literature, and science. Barnard's enduring mission is to provide an environment conducive to inquiry, learning, and expression while also fostering women's abilities, interests, and concerns.